Uneven Octagon

Uneven Octagon

Shahidul Alam

writers.ink

writers.ink
Concord Tower Suite 803
113 Kazi Nazrul Islam Avenue
Dhaka 1000, Bangladesh
Phone: 880-2-9335607
E-mail: naz@accesstel.net
       writers.ink@accesstel.net
Website: www.writersinkbd.com

First published 2007
Copyright © writers. ink

Cover design by Pradyut Kumar Das

ISBN 984 8715 07 X

All events and characters in these stories are fictional. Any resemblance is purely coincidental.

Distributed by The University Press Limited
Red Crescent House (6th Floor)
61 Motijheel C/A, Dhaka 1000
Tel: 880-2-956544, 880-2-9565443
Fax: 880-2-9565443
e-mail : upl@bttb.net.bd, upl@bangla.net
website: www.uplbooks.com

Published by Niaz Zaman, writers.ink, Dhaka 1000, Bangladesh. Printed at Mother Printers, 8, 10, Nilkhet, Babupura, Dhaka 1205, Bangladesh.

Contents

Angst and Ennui	1
The Student and the Bird Lady	25
Sajeda	39
Third World Exposition	55
Fitzrovia	67
Three Women — and a Bond	83
Notting Hill Nocturnal	101
Delusionals	115

Angst and Ennui

The tiny mouse was terrified. It had forgotten the gnawing hunger that had landed it in its current predicament. As mice go, it was an exception. Frail, with none of the sleek gray fur routinely on the fat well-fed variety, its thin ribs outlined themselves against a sickly pink skin, patches of which pathetically declared themselves through dull ash-coloured fur that was falling off. Not having been able to find food for several days, it was emaciated to the point where it could barely move on legs that were beginning to seem more appropriate for the bodies of the spindly spiders that infest the houses, grand and shanty alike, of Bangladesh. It had painfully propelled those legs towards the box that promised life: food! It had smelled the bits of the old cheese, chalk-coloured, juicy and full of holes that are peculiar to the region, and cooked rice inside the shoebox-sized rectangular wooden structure. With steps quickened a notch or two as it neared the structure's lip, and with listless whiskers perking up to produce one or two fluttering waggles at the impending prospect of nibbling and gorging, nibbling and gorging, gorging, gorging... growing fat and round and shiny and happy, happy, happy... when the world turned black around it with a hideous bang. The trap door had shut behind it.

The mouse froze as the pitch-black world around it exerted a mesmeric, terrifying pressure on that tiny body inside which the miniscule heart was thumping loudly and wildly. The little creature's eyes reflected its inner turmoil as they alternately froze into a blank stare and madly darted from one end of the sockets to the other. For a long time it stood paralyzed, unable and unwilling to move. Then its brain registered that the abysmal darkness had yielded ever so reluctantly to a diffusion of wan light struggling through the razor-thin spaces in the contraption. Once that registered, the tiny body made its first, hesitant movement — an exploratory foot forward. Assured that another bang was not forthcoming, it slowly moved to the nearest edge. A few moments of hesitation and then the transformation occurred. The smell of food was overpowering. Its lure was mesmerizing. The scrawny stomach turned in one last supreme effort to growl and succeeded in bringing out a barely audible squeak from the mouse. And, as if in a trance, that wasted body began to move. Really move. Not in the way that well-fed healthy mice move when in a hurry, a blur of gray gone before the blink of an eye, but in a gallop when compared to the snail-like pace it had geared up for moving towards the trap entrance.

The exertion caused it to delay in tucking into the fluffy white grains and the pockmarked, moist off-white sponginess. And then it did, first nibbling with painful deliberation the nearest grains of rice, only just beginning to lose their outer layer of moisture, and then, with a little more vigour, the grains that were strewn all around the base of the ragged piece of cheese. The mouse paused, taking a last check on the zing of its revitalizing energy and attacked. The two curved incisors cut into the soft, slightly rancid cheese, hesitatingly at first, as if making sure that it was not biting into a mirage, and then with urgency. Its sides bulged out, straining the ribs against the skin while one side of the cheese caved into a tiny sliver of new moon. The edges of the sharp incisors left their mark as the piece of cheese was whittled away. The creature stopped, trying to decide on fattening up against future famine or taking a nap before resuming the feast. Its cogitation was rudely interrupted by a loud screech followed by a shaft of bright light hitting it as if with physical force. And then it was tumbling downwards to hit the back wall of the trap and a large hairy hand was reaching for it. The mouse saw five stout naked branches coming towards it and an endless black forest covering the massive trunk that let out those sinister appendages. It cringed, and all the energy it had gained over the last several minutes could not induce it to move even a single muscle of its limbs. Its fright turned into terror at the sight of the face peering in with a clipped dark moustache shading a pair of thin lips and resting beneath a ferocious hawk-like nose and with a pair of piercing brown eyes taking stock from beneath a pair of neatly-groomed bushy black brows. And then that face began to grow larger and larger and the mouse's face changed into a face that was Wahidul Bari's and its eyes were bulging out into large petrified orbs and the mouth opened into a scream that would not come and then did, in bursts, and Wahidul Bari woke up in a sweat that poured out from all over his body in that stifling summer heat of August 1971.

He displayed the classic waking up on a nightmare characteristics: sitting up with a dazed expression and staying there as he struggled to decide on whether he was really awake or in the reality of his ghastly dreamland, then slowly looking around him as the realization dawned that the reality was the familiarity of his room whose faded yellow colour was given an artificial brightness by the rays of the morning sun, and then let his head droop to his chest in a simultaneous expression of relief that the nightmare was over and an inner dismay at the recollection of the devilish concoction of his brain. The air was sultry even at daybreak. Already the indications of an oppressively hot day were apparent to Wahid. The whirring overhead electric fan that had whirled all night at maximum speed, and was still in the same motion, had only circulated the same stale air around the room with monotonous regularity, offering some relief, but unable to dispel the sultry atmosphere inside. "God knows it is stuffy outside," Wahid thought sourly. "Wish I was in the big bedroom." Which happened to be his parents' room and which, most importantly, was equipped with an almost inaudibly purring air conditioner. "Got to have the damned fan oiled." It did emit a regular squeak at each revolution, but it was certainly not pronounced or annoying, but Wahid was in a foul mood. And he felt clammy. Finally he came out of his torpor and rushed to one of the two wide windows of his room. This one opened out to the manicured lawn that ended at the brick wall that marked the side boundary between his parents' house and the neighbour on its left. The window was closed, although the glass panes allowed the rays of the morning sun to blaze through. He now pushed out the panes after unlatching them from the inside and the fresh, though not crisp, outside air wafted in to take away some of the discomfort. It would not be long, though, before the air coming in would be uncomfortably hot and humid. Wahid momentarily clutched the solid iron bars that stood in the way of easy entry by burglars and other ill-intentioned people. They conveyed a sense of physical safety, but to Wahid, the bars were a symbolic prison of the free spirit. The neighbour's lawn with flowerbeds facing his family's house, he mused, created enough space between the two houses for free air flow and for the rising sun to bestow its rays inside his room. He looked down at the two rows of flowerbeds with their white lilies and red roses, took in their early morning fragrance, and turned his attention to the other window.

The other window was similar in build and structure to the one just opened, but it looked out over a shorter expanse of manicured lawn that ended at the edge of a four-metre high lime-washed plastered brick wall that marked the outer boundary of the premises. An asphalt road ran parallel to it, originating as a branch of the principal thoroughfare, Mirpur Road, and disappearing into a mesh of interconnecting byways outside Dhanmandi. The road, whose asphalt cover would gain the consistency of soft putty under the baking tropical sun, kept the window facing it in shade almost day and night, day after day after day, since March 26, 1971. From that day, to Wahid, it had become a road of fear. In itself, of course, it was not; it was most distinguishable by the number it had been given to assist residents of, and visitors to, the upscale Dhanmandi Residential Area. It was not even viewed as a road of fear by several residents of the rather modernistic, mostly two-storied, houses lining up in neat order on both its sides. And trees planted at regular intervals along its sides offered some shade and a lot of green view. It was pleasant in a pleasing part of Dhaka (then spelt Dacca) city, not a path of fear in a city of torment. Or was it? To Wahid it had been feeling that way for almost five months; before that, it had been his little corner of arcadia in what was really just a large town of a Third World country.

Wahid was one of the privileged youths of East Pakistan. There were not that many in that province in 1971 and, when counted in isolation from their non-Bengali counterparts, even less in number. A sizeable chunk had their schooling at St. Joseph's High, St. Gregory's High, Holy Cross High, Viqarunnessa High, St. Francis' High and an assortment of other English-medium schools that were spread out across the essentially large town called Dhaka, still with wide-open spaces within and between residential neighbourhoods in the late 1960s. The first two were for boys, the others for girls, and upon graduation, many young men headed for Notre Dame College while the young women sought admission at Holy Cross College. Except for Viqarunnessa, American Catholic missionaries ran the other institutions. That subtly set them apart from, and to their students, alum and their parents a cut above, the rest of the city schools. Viqarunnessa, however, for its academic excellence and with daughters of the city elite, was placed in the same hierarchy, contrived and more felt, but occasionally blurted out, by their students and their parents. And the constituents of this cluster of elitism usually interacted among themselves to emphasize their privileged station from the mammoth count of the others. This set was miniscule and their children, especially those reared in the English-medium environment, lived in a cocoon of their own reality built around the real and imagined culture of the West, the United States and Great Britain in particular, and in the ways of the modish city in West Pakistan, Karachi. It hardly took in the reality of the masses around them, in whom the seething economic and political discontent had been manifest for some time since the mid-1960s. And in the Bengalis was added the element of cultural disquiet, and a volatile mix in a characteristically emotionally charged people was beginning to build up into a volcanic eruption that threatened to cause a lot of damage to the existing structure of Pakistan.

Wahid was just beginning to understand the possible ramifications of the politically explosive situation obtaining in East Pakistan after he had become a freshman at Dhaka University's Economics department. That was in 1969 and none who was a student of that institution at that time could not but have been aware of the intensity of the political tsunami that was the province then because Dhaka University student activists had led from the front and pushed from the back in propelling the Bengalis towards becoming a nation seething to explode into one final statement of freedom. Those were heady days of endless rallies and speeches as the exuberance of youth in a normally intensely emotional population often compelled the elderly political leaders to throw the caution of advancing years to the winds and actually be led by the student hierarchs. They were in a zone where nothing was impossible and the moon was theirs for the asking. Wahid was never a participant in the mass display of discontent and expectation, but he could not avoid being touched by it, even if he had wanted to. But he wanted to. With a thrill he discovered that he was stirred and even dared to participate in the rallies and join in their rallying cries. But years of indifference to the everyday whopping reality around him and his long existence in a cocooned state instinctively held him back from taking part in the grimy street stomping.

Wahid had a dreamlike existence at St. Joseph's. Only that was his reality. His father was a highly successful lawyer in a country with a noticeably litigious population. Their litigious propensity in no way approaches the amazing range and mission of the Americans, but they make a sizeable contribution to the judicial system all right, a part of which is done under-the-counter. And, quite in keeping with an economy primarily based on agriculture, especially in the pre-1971 years, land and landed property disputes are the principle issues of litigation. A number of them are petty and ridiculous, but the litigants go at it for years, and not a few end up being penniless from a position of at least some wealth. The lawyers make merry and one gets rich at the expense of another's necessity, misery and, every so often, pure folly. Wahid's father was a wealthy legal counselor who had spurned the offer of being a High Court Justice on the ground that he earned in a couple of days what his monthly salary would be, and he had to take into account the upbringing of his three daughters and two sons and maintain his comfortable lifestyle, and that cost money. And his inner self kept assuring him that he loved the sight, smell (of the crisp new notes) and feel of money. Wahid was his second born, two years younger than his doted-upon and doting daughter. The alternating pattern was repeated with a daughter following a son following a daughter following Wahid. Lawyers and landowners constituted the bulk of the leading political elements during the days of Pakistan, but Mr. Bari, while holding political views, was not interested in serving the people's interests.

If his father held political views, Wahid in his school and college days thought of politics as a pastime indulged in by demagogues craving attention. He knew that Ayub Khan, imposing and handsome, was the president, Monem Khan, unimposing and with leg-wrapping pajamas, sherwani, an ever-present astrakhan hat on his head and black-rimmed glasses, was the governor of East Pakistan, the fierce-looking Nawab with a grand moustache was the governor of West Pakistan, the paunchy, long-bearded Maulana Bhashani with a ubiquitous indigenous round cap on his head was a rabble rouser and...well, he did not know, or care to, about anyone else. He lived in a large modern house with his own room, lacked for nothing by way of contemporary things that had high status stamped on them, had good friends, went to the numerous American and English movies that were shown at Naz, Modhumita, Balaka and Gulistan, attended jam sessions where local rock and roll bands like The Windy Side of Care, The Rambling Stones, The Lightnings, and the occasional visiting West Pakistani groups performed, played cricket, basketball and softball, frequented the Chinese restaurants, drove around in the family car and chatted with his younger sister's friends, one of whom he fancied as his girlfriend. Life was a reflection of American culture, not an exact image, but a serviceable replica. Life was good. Wahid performed creditably in his Cambridge O-level examinations and went to Notre Dame College for his Intermediate studies.

At Notre Dame, as 1968 gave way to 1969, and his final exams were approaching, he had his first whiff of agitational politics. It was nothing much, just a bunch of students shouting some slogans about something or the other. One of which he distinctly remembered was the demand for Ayub's removal from power. He noticed that almost the entire group came from Bengali-medium high schools. None of his friends were participating in it. He had an up close and personal look at the face of sloganeering march as he was literally engulfed within it. He was about to walk to the entrance of the main building when the marchers came out of it, and he found himself being carried forward by it, back-pedaling part of the way and then synchronizing with the direction of the march by simply making an about turn. He noticed a few of his classmates around him, people he saw in class but with whom he did not remember ever having exchanged a word. Wahid's friends were the Bengali and non-Bengali boys who had graduated from his and other English-medium high schools of the city. Then he noticed that the marchers beamed at him, or appeared to, privileged to have one of the "in-people" of the campus in their midst. Some actually talked to him, and he made some mindless, but harmless, noncommittal remarks. Extraordinary! Very soon the march reached the college entrance gate and Wahid made his escape, going back to his friends to entertain them with the tale of his little adventure. Then they went back to their normal fare of discussing girls, the latest fashion, parties, movies, rock LPs, all things American, and all such things that distinguished them from the marchers and their ilk in college.

Wahid felt more in common with the non-Bengali in-crowd than with the Bengali-medium Bengalis of his college. He, along with the other hip crowd, thought of them, when he thought of them at all, as uncouth and bucolic. He dressed in the latest fashion, all psychedelic, wore long hair, drooping moustache and John Lennon sunglasses, and made his weekly pilgrimage to the Hotel Intercontinental (now Sheraton), that big pleasure dome for the rich and the jet set in a generally quiet big town whose tranquility was frequently broken, as the 1960s segued into the 1970s, by bursts of rallies, sloganeering and agitation. That set was small, had an air about it, and was snobbish, but its members had genteel manners that distinguished them from any nouveau riche who might want to belong through the power of new money. Family background, good breeding, and old money would make a determined effort to keep their social distance from the "wrong" family background and new money. So Wahid kept to his crowd, although it was diluted in a larger mix of students at the college level, safely negotiated the IA final exams and performed well enough to get admitted to one of the coveted departments of Dhaka University.

Economics was a challenge, but even more was the adjustment to life in a public university. Wahid had only gone to exclusive private institutions with a number of American educators; now he was among the Notre Dame-type hoi polloi multiplied several times over. Actually the college *Bangoos* were cultivated compared to the cultivators' sons and daughters and other bumpkins who were his fellow students. He realized with deep anguish that he was now an outsider and in an alien world. And, for almost a year, he made no effort to meld in that world. He found assurance in the small number of English-medium background students, several of whom were themselves looking to exist in a cocoon of elitism surrounded by a sea of restless pastoral Bengalis. Wahid witnessed from close proximity the seemingly endless processions of emotionally charged students belonging to a variety of front organizations of political parties chanting a common theme: economic and political justice for the Bengalis. He was beginning to understand the deeper emotions of the students, although he could not bring himself up to getting involved with them. His life was a mix of classroom, exclusive set of friends, parties, and a girlfriend. She was a freshman in the English department, a daughter of an air force officer, with a less-familiar English-medium coeducational Shaheen School and very familiar Holy Cross College background, pretty without being beautiful, with enchanting eyes that confused as much as they revealed.

Wahid was totally in love with her and gradually started restricting his time for his friends. Large-town Dhaka and seething Dhaka University were forgotten in a frenzied existence of telephone calls, lunch dates at Chinese restaurants, talk, talk, talk, and stolen kisses in the under-construction top floor of the university. Petting soon followed, but the two could not go any further. He wanted to — he could smuggle her to his bedroom or his old school friend Fakrul's —

but she did not subscribe to the free sex message of the 1960s. The days went by like a dream and even his university seemed to shed its agitational cloak as Yahya Khan declared a schedule for holding general elections. There was a hiccup when the central government was accused by the Bengalis of callousness in handling the aftermath of the devastating tidal bore and cyclone of November 1970 that snuffed out an estimated half a million Bengali lives. But the growling soon subsided as the elections were around the corner and the people got busy preparing for a victory of their demand for a just and equitable society based on Bengali nationalism. Curiously, Wahid became better acquainted with the classmates he had largely shunned for over a year and got a real feel for the underlying currents of this nationalism. He was not sure about his own feelings on the subject, but he definitely felt strongly that East Pakistan should be an autonomous unit and that its economic and political demands should be satisfied by the central government. Gradually he realized that he was on the fringes of the Dhaka University crowd and thought it was not a bad thing either. He felt relief at the unconscious lifting of a heavy millstone.

The elections came and went, and Bengali nationalism gained a massive vote of confidence. Dhaka and the university rejoiced and Yahya assured transfer of power on time to Sheikh Mujibur Rahman and his Awami League. The Bengalis exalted even more. Dhaka was a festive and happy big town. Wahid was watching a cricket match between Pakistan and a visiting Commonwealth team at the Dhaka stadium in February 1971 when the joy went out of the Bengalis and the lights went out on Bengali dreams and aspirations. The provincial capital exploded and carried the rest of the province with it. He noticed the mood change in the Bengalis while returning from the truncated game in the company of a mass of humanity that swelled as it moved along, and he along with it, until, as it approached Dhaka University, it had grown into an ocean of growling and angry humanity. From small and large rallies of festive Bengalis in eager anticipation of better days ahead that were going to be shaped by their own, the seething mass now raged and menaced in frustration at having its lawfully gained prize rudely snatched away by Yahya's declaration. For the next few weeks Wahid was caught in a limbo of not knowing what to do and expect. Dhaka (and the province) was a unit with only a façade of a government structure, but no effective government, and yet, strangely, not experiencing the kind of sweeping anarchy that could logically be expected in the near state of nature that it had reverted to.

These were strange days because a de facto administration based on directives from the Bengali leaders and the victorious party were operational, in however pell-mell fashion, while the de jure authority turned into a spectacle of irrelevance. Because the center of authority had reverted to the people and its exploding nationalism, only their leaders were able to maintain the semblance of order that existed, but their pent-up emotions were sporadically let loose in lawlessness and violence. That made Dhaka an uncertain place in March 1971. The risk of getting hurt physically was patent, especially after dark. And so the night owl Wahid gave up, or was forced to give up, his nocturnal visitation to friends; the Chinese restaurants were mostly closed at night, the Intercontinental existed in a trance of anomaly, and the night parties had been put on an extended hold. Some terrible happening hung in the air and was openly discussed, including in the Bari household. The family decided to keep a low profile about the existing situation and likely outlook with friends and relatives, because Mr. Bari favoured a constitutional settlement while most of the rest of the Bengalis seemed determined to go into armed confrontation to realize their demands which, as March rolled with heated fury towards April, now meant independence. Mr. Bari could not be sure about anyone else's true feelings and thought it prudent, for him and his family, to be as non-committal as possible when the subject matter came up, as it inevitably did, in the company of relatives, friends and neighbours. His practice had become a shadow of its hitherto extremely busy and lucrative self, and he had enough leisure time to make, and entertain, diurnal visits and visitations from people also caught up in an existence of uncertainty and worry. He was careful to return not too long after sundown at the latest and instructed his children to do the same.

Wahid spent much of his daytime at home, his spirit muzzled, and consoled himself with talking endlessly over the phone with Shaheen, his girlfriend, and taking in the occasional visit of his Bengali friends. Many of the non-Bengali friends, of affluent houses and fearing trouble, had left for West Pakistan. He had made one or two visits to the university, which had closed down seemingly on its own volition, and found it a living organism of anticipation of freedom, fear of the unknown, restlessness to be doing something to accelerate the process towards having it out, and talk, talk, talk. He listened to a lot of that from the two or three of the number of classmates he had started cultivating outside his usual crowd. They had no answers, but a lot of questions, mostly rhetorical, a mix of excitement and fear, but one surging outburst of emotion: the time had come for a confederated Pakistan or independent Bangladesh.

And, meanwhile, army reinforcements were arriving to add to the lonely 14 Division that had been allocated the defence of East Pakistan. Wahid had long wondered about that: a mere division to thwart the aggressive thrust of a much more numerically superior Indian force? The theory held by the central government that the defence of East Pakistan lay in having a forceful military establishment in West Pakistan he considered to be illogical. He had mulled over the subject off and on since the 1965 Indo-Pak war, and always concluded that he was naked and desperately busy trying to cover his genitalia with his hands, leaving him hamstrung, and his adversary closing in from all sides to take him a prisoner. Hell, his province was a prisoner of imposed inadequacy. And now soldiers were steadily arriving and were being subjected to a generally hostile reception. The occasional confrontation between the two inevitably occurred with the people getting visibly divided between the small non-Bengali settlers and the Bengalis. This could not go on like this, reflected Wahid, now that he had so much time for reflection. Something had to give.

And it did, on the night of 25 March 1971. It was one of those events that induce the question of exactly what one was doing at the particular time of the happening. Wahid could tell his grandchildren that he was sitting on the loo, defecating, before turning himself in for a long night's sleep. The next day he was meeting Shaheen at Fakrul's house. The university was out of the question, his parents were now around most of the time and he drew the line at being brazen in their face. Visiting her at her place was out of the question (her mother would blow her top, damage her daughter's eardrums and maybe have him horsewhipped by the house-guard). So to Fakrul's it was decided; he lived with his married elder brother, they were all broad-minded, and his friend was libidinous and often had the house to himself to indulge in his concupiscence. Maybe he would get lucky the next day. His raging hormones were boiling with the long days of ennui and inaction.

Wahid was going to have a long night's sleep to fine tune his batteries for next forenoon's action. As he drifted off he dreamt of being engulfed by a staccato of sound of popping fireworks. The image of Shab-e-Barat and the lighting of an assortment of homemade crackers imposed themselves on his slumbering brain and he found it all a little irritating and he woke up and there was no Shab-e-Barat and no fireworks, but more insistent steady chatters interspersed with metallic cracks and loud booms until a huge exploding ball of bright light invaded through his open windows and a terrifying single boom followed and he thought that his eardrums had burst and the end of the world had begun. Instinctively, he scurried under his bed and clamped his ears to shut out the sounds of annihilation. He wanted to close out the flashes of light, too, but he was petrified in his position, his limbs unwilling to move to shut the windows and have the heavy curtains cover them. He found himself praying to a God he had only sought the assistance of when in tight situations and this was the tightest one he had ever been in.

Surely, God could not destroy the earth so soon; it was so young; scientists said so; the Prophet had preached Islam a mere thirteen centuries ago and the religion needed thousands of years to spread even more; and he was so young and he had no time to perform Hajj and atone for all the sins he had accumulated and he loved his parents and brother and sisters even though the eldest was on his case while she went about gallivanting with guys (he saw her at the TSC and kept mum in spite of her big sister attitude) and...please God make this thing go away and at least let him and his family live. And then from far, far, far away he heard his father calling him to come to the living room but he did not pay any attention until he felt the tug on his arm and turned his head to peer into the impressionist face of his dad — at least, in the gloom, it felt like something out of an impressionist master. He crawled after his upright father, out of the door and into the center of the ample and tastefully furnished living room. He completed the entire circle that had assembled there on the assumption that it was the safest place in the house. Even the servants were there. They all crouched behind two heavy sofas that had been dragged to the center of the room. Not the servants, though. They bunched up near the door opening to the inner part of the house. And, for a long time, as the din went on outside, no one spoke. The only words were recitations from the Holy Koran, as each sought salvation for his/her soul and beseeched Allah to stop the terrible whatever outside and not take away their souls so abruptly.

All became aware of the silence descending around them as the early dawn filtered through the inner diaphanous white curtains that were meant to keep insects out and gently ripple and waft with the incoming breeze. One or two of them later recalled the intensity of the gunfire and thunderous explosions — all had fairly early realized that that is exactly what they were — abating to the sporadic crackle and brief rat-tat-tats until silence roared into existence. All checked to see that everyone was alive and unhurt and conversation began haltingly and in sotto voce. The first few minutes were spent in assuring each other that the army had struck and in speculating about its targets, which took the level of the conversation to some wild assertions, high-pitched voices and animated gesticulations. Nothing was resolved and Wahid's mother decided to have breakfast served and call up relatives and friends to find out about their and the city's condition. The early summer sun had long cleared the horizon and Wahid became aware of the movement of people in front of his house. They were curious neighbours and people he did not recognize, almost all in shirts and lungis, young, middle-aged and old, moving along the street, the bewildered and anxious looks on their faces clearly visible across the short distance of the lawn in front of their living room.

Wahid had his breakfast and, around eleven, only telling his father that he would have a look around the vicinity and visit a friend or two in the area, went out. He had no intention of visiting any friend, but, nonetheless, ran into Salim. They walked through a city of fear and blood. And dead bodies and armed military personnel with guns drawn and hard and suspicious looks. The two friends met at the top of the road leading away from the Dhanmandi lake bridge and bifurcating around the massive walled sports field with its modest Dhanmandi Club house positioned adjacent to a lone towering *taal*-palm tree until separately meeting the Mirpur road. Wahid would have been perfectly happy to have strolled around within the Dhanmandi area and taken a long distance peek across the lake at Sheikh Mujib's house because he had figured out that the terrifying chatters and blasts of the night had come from that direction. In the event, he did not, as some irresistible force drew him towards New Market and his university. He was sure that Mujib had been killed. How couldn't he be, if the army had shot dead his Dhanmandi friends? Salim and Wahid found out about that as soon as they reached the Dhanmandi ground area and saw several bodies lying around, their eyes half-closed and looking as dead as a dead fish's eyes do, arms outstretched like the depictions of Jesus Christ pinned to the cross, the congealed blood beginning to get malodorous in the intense heat and attracting those ubiquitous iridescent bluish-green houseflies. They would have a feast, Wahid thought sourly, after overcoming the shock and horror of seeing for the first time bodies riddled with bullets, the pinkish-red flesh exposed through torn skin for all to see and to be fascinated or to recoil with repulsion, and a couple were his friends. He had played cricket with them, they were from the area, and were the sons of upper class Bengalis. And now they were lying with other Bengalis like rickshaw-pullers who might have strained their legs to carry them in their vehicles to their destination, with the transaction of labour payment ending any interaction between them. And for what? Being Bengalis? Wahid began to feel anger welling up from deep within him. These people did not have to die like that. Not his friends, not the others. Involuntarily he was being propelled through the roads interconnecting Dhanmandi to Road No. 3, and out on to Mirpur road towards New Market and off towards Dhaka University.

Tikka Khan had been let loose on the Bengalis. Wahid saw the evidence everywhere as he walked almost in a trance down Mirpur Road, past Balaka Cinema Hall, took a left on Nilkhet Road at one end of New Market, went past the Nilkhet police barracks, strolled and stopped near Iqbal Hall, looked at the Arts Building from afar, debating whether to head in that direction or take a right on Fuller Road, eventually deciding on first going past the British Council, taking a quick glance on his right at the eastern side of SM Hall, turning left until he arrived at the outer walls of Jagannath Hall and took in the scene before him. Here he lingered for about fifteen minutes, found himself going round and past the UOTC building, the TSC, took a left between the University Library and Public Library building complexes and Rokeya Hall until he was standing in front of the Arts Building. The evidence was in the hard, suspicious and menacing faces of the battle-geared army men in their vehicles and on the ground, on the bullet-pocked walls and buildings, shattered structures, the smoldering police barrack, the smell of recently fired ammunition, the patches of metallic blood, and the bodies. Wahid smelled their death, saw their lifelessness. They were multiplied several times over those he had left behind in his posh residential area. The smell of death was that of the freshly sacrificed cattle and goats at Eid-ul-Azha; its sight left him in a state between reality and abstraction. He had seen images of the Vietnam War, of the Viet Cong at the moment of being publicly executed by the Vietnamese senior police officer, of footages on the TV news bulletins, but none of that had prepared him for the actual sight of violent death and destruction. People were moving along, not that many, but not too few either, looking around, stopping and directing surreptitious glances at the soldiers. They were mostly silent, moving like zombies, letting out the occasional sound, their dazed looks and horrified faces uniting them in an unspoken bond of humanity witnessing the destruction of a part of humanity, of themselves. Somewhere along the way, John Donne pulsed through Wahid's mind: "No man is an Iland, intire of itselfe... any mans death diminishes me... And therefore never send to know for whom the bell tolls; It tolls for thee." They kept up a refrain throughout his hurried walk back the same way to the shelter of his house and family. Only he was not sure if they were a shelter. The bullets and the men shooting them decided on shelter. And, therefore, Dhaka became a prison for those who stayed inside and a suffocating entity from which to escape for those who could not take it anymore, even if it meant chancing death.

Wahid and his family resigned themselves to God and their home for seeing them through with their lives intact. Their souls had already taken a battering of reality check. Wahid wondered how much he would be changed once this nightmare was over. That it would be over he had no doubt whatsoever. Nothing is forever, except death. And that, according to some religions, was not forever either. Maybe death would not claim him. Hell, he was becoming too morbid, was thinking too much. His idle thoughts, though, were not turning into the devil's workshop. They were getting angry, frustrating, with no sign of relief. Most of the time he stayed to himself, within the prison that was his room, dark and gloomy most of the day, now that heavy curtains permanently prevented sunlight from coming through the front windows and only a few hours were allowed the side windows to have their draperies pushed aside, open out to a sight of green lawn, flower beds, low wall and one side of a house. The maidservant carried out the ritual of allowing in sunlight and air, or dampness and air, well into the morning, and closing them out well before sunset. Wahid was in his room for only a short time during this freshening-up period. The front windows were also opened and shut during those hours, but the curtains covering them would not be pulled back. Because the road ran in front, and over the asphalt sped military jeeps and troop carriers. They were frequent during April, and then became sporadic, but did not altogether disappear. The sight of the armed troops with mean unsmiling looks unnerved and depressed him. He did not want to see them more than was inevitable. Certainly he had a choice of shutting them out from his front window. And his mother insisted that a swathed window would not interest the soldiers in having a look-see at the occupant inside. Her eldest son was liable to behaving wildly, like ogling at the troops through the window. Of all her children she was most worried about his safety in the days when very few were safe.

His mother was way off about one thing. Wahid had no intention of staring at the soldiers. In fact, he avoided looking at them on encountering them during his measured wanderings out of his house. Those became more and more rationed as the months dragged on through the hot summer, the sweltering monsoon and the early winter as his friends and acquaintances started disappearing. One day they were there, the next they had vanished without ever having informed him about their destination. Their parents would talk vaguely about them having gone to their village home to live with relatives and in a couple of cases, the entire family had disappeared with his acquaintance, leaving only an old servant or a *darwan* to look after the empty house and give it a stamp of occupation. "Things are not good here," they would tell him, "they are safe in the village." This was in August, when, paradoxically, the sustained curfew from March 26 onwards had long been relaxed and there was hardly any visible presence of uniformed soldiers during the daytime. But, Wahid heard, there were a lot of military intelligence men in civilian clothes around, and an even greater number of civil intelligence people looking for the Mukti Bahini and sympathizers of Bangladesh. There were stories of late night calls at houses, pick up of suspects, mostly young men, and tales of terrifying torture cells and dead bodies making the random appearance in different parts of the city. There were accounts of young women in army camps, of some at least belonging to middle-class families. They were almost all Muslims, but the army thought otherwise until the males' dicks were checked and their acumen in reciting from the Holy Koran was assessed, but the females had no way of being physically distinguished from the Hindus who they were often accused of being, or sympathizing with. But women were women and religion was not exactly an impediment to enjoying them. Wahid recalled his lovely sisters, his aristocratic mother, their belonging to the society's thin upper crust, and shuddered. No wonder Dhaka was thinning out each day. The Hindus, those still alive, had long crossed the borders into India. One of his Hindu school friends and his father had been riddled with bullets in their stately home on the very first night of carnage. The rest of his family had fled to Kolkata and the sanctuary of relatives. But far more Muslims had sought shelter across the borders, several to have a good time, and come back with the hallowed credential of being a Mukti Bahini just on the strength of having stepped across a border, a lot more to join the guerilla force to fight for the right to their homeland that was now Bangladesh in their hearts, whether it had any UN sanction of approval or not.

Wahid's father's practice had gone down considerably, but his ample savings plus the rent money coming in from his family house in Rankin Street enabled them to live in comfort without being able to indulge in the accessories of that comfort. He had ample time to mull over things, sometimes thinking of taking his family across the border and joining the steady exodus of people that would peak at 10 million. But inertia set in after every one of his cogitations, the familiarity of home gave him an illusion of security, and he stayed in place till the material end of Pakistan in Bangladesh. But he did make his wish known to the persons he visited or who visited him and unconsciously making a nationalistic statement for a politically apathetic man. The astute and successful lawyer also saw Dhaka wearing a deserted look, a cloak of terror and foreboding of something more terrible waiting to happen, of night curfews, bursts of explosives and the chatter of automatic weapons that spoke of guerilla activity, of a ghost town at night when all stayed in and turned in early and the silence of the empty streets broken by the occasional roar of military vehicles on patrol to enforce the curfew or on other missions, of listless faces on the normally animated and smiling Bengali, of the unspoken fear of a knock on the door in the dead of night, of shops opening late and closing early, of the almost total absence of females on the streets, of...the rest is over to his son.

Wahid was feeling crushed by having nothing to do. He lost all urge to read, finding the endless time too boring to devote to a book, but having little alternatives to make it palatable. The diminishing circle of friends and acquaintances was becoming a burden, talking over the phone with his girlfriend a tribulation to be endured each day two or three times, the campus was a moss-infested forlorn, and forbidding, structure, and his family a boring group that he had to suffer day in and day out. His visits grew shorter, his conversations tongue-tied, his moping grew longer and he longed to scream at — at everybody and nothing, at God, at Yahya, Niazi, his friends, family, neighbours, the soldiers, the guerillas, the beastly weather, Dhaka, the list was a specific concoction of the specific moment when his brain felt like bursting and he taking a light machine gun on the one hand and a sub-machinegun in the other and blowing everyone and everything in sight to smithereens. Dhaka was killing him; he wanted to kill it first. Its walls were closing in on him from all sides and he could feel the steely fingers of asphyxiation approaching his throat. He had to blast that threat away. But how could he do that in a stifling atmosphere that sapped away one's energy and chopped away at one's spirit?

Wahid had to get acquainted with the guerilla friends of a few of his acquaintances. These were his university classmates that he had made the effort to know during the last days of a vibrant and iconoclastic campus. That was, oh so many thousands of years ago. He had no idea what he was going to do when he met them except that somehow the fact of the meeting would replace his existence as a cornered (and a little frightened) rat with some thrill and give his life a reason to go on. That was in mid-September, a little over a month after his horrifying nightmare, when the season was subtly changing and the rain and the heat began to fluctuate from day to day, occasionally from hour to hour. The feel of distant winter, lovely winter, was in the air in a Dhaka of wide-open spaces, low structures, and a curious intimacy. The guerilla operations had gained in urgency as was reported by All-India Radio, to which he and his family listened every day, several times a day, with ears glued close to the Grundig, tuned down low, in the comparative safety of the interior room of the house, the eldest girl's bedroom. The BBC and Voice of America broadcasts also spoke of the increase, although with more realistic assessments and commentaries, and PTV Dhaka gave away the escalation by referring almost daily to body counts of "miscreants" (the Pakistani version of Mukti Bahini guerillas) killed in encounters all over the country. Wahid used to listen to the still nights sporadically shattered by short bursts of gunfire and the booms of plastic explosives going off. The wide-open spaces and the silence of the curfew in operation made those sounds appear closer than they were, but Wahid was reassured. Something was going to happen to end his existential being. Then the dogs would once again bark, the crows would caw to their hearts' content, the brown kites would let out their piercing screech, and all would be right with the world. The vultures would no longer fatten themselves on the fallen. The dogs were afraid to bark, the crows and kites must have sought sanctuary away from Dhaka, and their silence made him realize just how much they were a part of his life. He just took them for granted, and he wanted them back to become an unnoticed part of him. How he hated that silence, the muted daytime sounds, the stillness of the long dark nights spent in vacantly staring at the black-and-white TV set until it was time for an early family dinner where talk was at a premium and the silence broken mainly by slurping noises and clinking cutlery, and an early turning in after all the doors and windows were secured tight (not much use if the late night call came, Wahid thought, we all live on so much hope and delusion) and the lights turned out inside the house.

Wahid finally made the connection he was looking for. They were about his age, with long hair in the fashion of the times (he had that too) and a scraggly beard often accompanying a drooping Mexican moustache, another contemporary fashion (he was clean shaven, but sported pronounced sideburns). They were from middle class and lower middle class backgrounds, were Intermediate, Degree and Dhaka University students (of departments other than Economics, and Wahid could not recall ever having seen them), and most lived in the Shantinagar area. Soon he was frequenting their houses and gaining their confidence. He might presently be able to persuade them to help him cross over to India to join one of the guerilla training camps. "All in good time," was all he got for an answer. His mother noticed his frequent absence from home, mostly during lunchtime, expressed her worries to him ("these aren't good times"), and received the reassuring answer of whiling away his time with university buddies to relieve himself of boredom ("I'm always home by sundown, aren't I?"). But someone in his neighbourhood obviously kept a tab on him and his movements because his father called him a few days later:

"What do you do with your time these days? Where do you go? Don't trust anyone. Stay home."

He could not stay home, but he could not tell his father the real reason why, and gave him the same answer that he gave his mother. But his father was dead right on the point of trust. Claustrophobic Dhaka, in spite of having thinned out, was made more unbearable by the growth of suspicion. Friends were suspect as were neighbours; even close relatives. No one could be sure of anyone else; no one could be sure of trusting another with his/her life. Dhaka had become a place of intrigue and suspicion, and its inhabitants victims or perpetrators of double-dealings and denunciations. Wahid felt trapped inside a place that he was born in and had grown to love. He could empathize with the mouse of his nightmare. He vowed to himself to be nice to mice in the future.

October was ready to give way to November and the winter chill was no longer a distant prospect, when the guerillas gave him the green signal to get ready to make the trek across the border. Dhaka regained its old esteem in his eyes. He was going to come back and relieve it of the vice-like grip that was choking the essence out of it. The old town, the very soul of the place, now physically and psychologically pulverized into a shell of its former self, would give off all the odours that made it unique, its inhabitants would become Dhakaias again, Dhanmandi and Gulshan would become unabashed havens for the snobs, the stray dogs would bark, the kites would swoop down to carry off chicks, and the crows would create a ruckus throughout the waking hours. Wahid would walk the campus, re-discover love and resume being Wahid. He would be free.

In November Wahid was in a small room of four solid walls, with no windows and a solid wooden door regulating entry and exit. He had no idea exactly where he was except that he was in excruciating pain and terrified. He had just undergone a variety of tortures carried out by a couple of *jawans* as a tall, angular handsome Punjabi major asked him questions that he was unable to answer. Some he did not know the answer to, others he could not answer because to do so truthfully would mean jeopardizing his friends' and acquaintances' lives. The officer was cool, cold, relentless, his methods mean and brutal. Wahid was bleeding and torn and swollen — and on his knees. He silently prayed to Allah as images of his parents and siblings raced across his mind. The knock on the door had come rather early — just as the family was finishing dinner — and Wahid's ears still rang with his mother's shrieks, his father's pleadings, and his siblings' wailings. As he turned around to take a last look at them before being forced into the pickup where three other unknown Bengalis were sitting tightly huddled in the face of several sub-machine guns pointed at their stomachs, he wished they had shot him dead so he did not have to hear the screams. He could not force back a steady stream of tears as the vehicle moved away from the familiarity of his house, his mother's wild eyes, his father's open mouth, and his siblings' thrashing arms.

The single bulb burned into Wahid as he lay spread-eagled on the floor, too weak to move after three days of deprived sleep, no food, sips of water at long intervals, non-stop questioning and the torture. There was such a variety and he had become numb to them after some time, drifting in and out of consciousness and not knowing what he told his interrogators. He was past caring, was seeing things that his beat-up brain wanted him to see. Now he saw through a haze the major standing behind a man with a large face dominated by a ferocious hawk-like nose over a pair of neatly clipped military moustache, who was leaning over him and peering at him with a pair of piercing brown eyes from under a groomed pair of bushy black brows. Then Wahid drifted off into unconsciousness as the military doctor's massive hairy forearms zeroed in with a large syringe towards a vein in his left arm and expertly pushed in the big needle. Wahid felt his heart grow larger and larger and the world in front of him smaller and smaller and the faces of his parents and siblings flashed in and out, in and out, in and out until all the lights went out with one final burst of incandescence. Then all was black. The doctor checked on the gargantuan syringe of blood that he had just sucked out. The major was thinking with satisfaction of the Pakistani lives that would be saved with the Bengali's blood.

The Student and the Bird Lady

Faisal used to run into the old woman and get disconcerted. Almost unfailingly. And invariably wonder. About that sour-faced, cantankerous bag lady — as she appeared to him — who somehow managed to put him ill at ease simply by being within his sight. And he positively quailed when he was in close proximity and earnestly wished that their moment of juxtaposition would be the briefest possible and that he would be able to rapidly put distance between himself and the object of his discomfiture. But he was fascinated. For as much as Faisal wanted to avoid her, he was equally drawn towards that old woman. If it was possible, he would have spied on her from around corners and hiding places without running the slightest risk of being seen in return. But he could not realistically try to conceal himself around street and building corners without arousing suspicion and unwanted attention from others. They would be perfectly justified, he reasoned, in classifying him as a lunatic or a criminal. And he was neither.

Faisal Qureshi was a graduate student in Business Administration at Boston University. In 1992, the year he had arrived in the United States from Karachi, Pakistan, he had just turned thirty. Besides trying to get his MBA degree, he would try to land a cushy job in the land of opportunity and permanently settle there. He would marry an American, preferably white, to hasten his objective of obtaining the Holy Grail of a green card. If a white were not available, a Hispanic or an East Asian or even a South Asian would do. But no blacks, or African-Americans as they were termed. He was not going to break the taboo imposed by his acquired prejudice. Other Pakistanis had obtained their green cards that way. Unlike some of them at least, he did not have a wife and one or two kids tucked away somewhere in distant Pakistan, waiting for the husband and father to come back, and waiting and waiting....

Faisal was a rather heavily-built man of medium height with swarthy features dominated by a bulbous aquiline nose, a full sensuous upper lip clamping down hard on a slightly thinner lower one, a pair of bushy eyebrows almost joined in a straight line above a pair of light brown eyes set wide apart in deep sockets, and a head of black curly hair carefully brushed back. When he first arrived, he possessed a clipped military moustache, which, he believed, added dash and panache to a manly appearance. Until paranoia took hold of him and, one morning, he shaved it off and, thereby, drew attention and comments to himself from friends and classmates. A perfectly innocent inquiry from a fellow-student, an American who he had first made acquaintance with about a month into the Fall semester, made him reintroduce the razor to the hairy growth between his nose and upper lip. He was asked about the Arab country he supposedly belonged to. Faisal was not particularly fond of Arabs, and he certainly did not wish to be identified as one. "It must be the moustache," he thought. It made him look Arab, although other people, on first meeting him, had thought him to be an Indian, or a Pakistani. Then it dawned on him that the Gulf War was a recent memory and the United States was still in the throes of a jingoistic patriotism. What if an American called him an Iraqi? He conjured up all the horrific ramifications of that and he decided the moustache must pay the price of his paranoia.

Faisal had actually first run into the bag lady of his future waking nightmares while the moustache still adorned his face. Having never been outside his country, he was nervous at having to become international in that vast land of opportunity, riches and freedom, the United States, no less. He had read much about it, heard even more, and seen it a whole lot on screen, mini and maxi. It looked so magical to his eyes that his heart dismissed the somewhat discordant picture that was painted by some of the literature and a few of the people he had talked to. But all that theoretical knowledge did not dispel the butterflies in his stomach that fluttered furiously as his aircraft touched down at Logan Airport. A couple of Pakistani friends, already studying at Boston University, helped him settle down, and he started life as a graduate student from his furnished studio in Beacon Street. The studio was part of a complex of apartments that Boston University had bought as part of its drive to acquire more real estate. They mostly housed its graduate students, and Faisal found himself on the ground floor looking out on famed Beacon Street and, beyond it, the even more recognized Fenway Park, where the Boston Red Sox baseball team lifted the spirits, and, every so often, broke the hearts, of its long-suffering fans.

For the first few days after he had moved in, Faisal used to peek out of his window and watch the women in their shorts walking to and away from the stadium, as the baseball season was winding down, and lusted for them. Since he could not physically have them, he consoled himself by frequently masturbating with their image in his mind. And then he had his first glimpse of the old crone. That is how she appeared when he almost ran into her that Friday morning. School was to start the following Monday, and he was going over to the bookstore for some essential purchase. He had just stepped out onto the small hallway when he had to hurriedly skid to a stop to avoid bumping into the tiny old lady pushing an empty shopping cart in front of her.

Her size was the first thing that struck Faisal. And, considering the subsequent impression that she created on him, the most misleading. He saw a wizened woman, well over seventy, hardly five feet tall, barely clearing the height of the cart she was pushing. Her wrinkled skin did its best to protect the desiccated flesh that gave shape to a brittle-looking skeleton and the gnarled claws that tightly gripped the cart handle provided an illusion of the talons of a medium-sized bird of prey. Old veins stuck out of her hands and lower legs like blue earthworms, and she looked hard at Faisal with rheumy watery-blue eyes that accused from beneath thin white eyebrows. The ancient wrinkled lips were thin, but if one let one's imagination open up even a little, one could easily visualize a very pretty mouth, that bewitched and beckoned, a long time ago, before time exacted its gradual, but relentless and merciless, toll. So was her petite body, which, now almost emaciated, suggested that it once held a slender voluptuousness in days long passed.

The old body and the old face had thin strands of hair, straining to cover the chicken neck and cut in a fringe just above the albino-like eyebrows, dyed a rich chestnut-brown, probably as an homage to the original colour of what could have been a luxuriant head of hair. If one dared to look at her long enough, one could also notice garish pink lipstick smeared over the gash of her small mouth. Then the effect of the blotchy-skinned body in its winter, with eyes gradually losing their light of life, vainly struggling to spread an illusion of spring about it through pink lips and coloured hair, compelled an effect of derision, pity, even revulsion, in viewers. But if one managed to see beyond the effects of time, one could envision a young woman of beauty, attracting the constant attention of men, perhaps giving in to some, but breaking the hearts of many. Actually Faisal did reflect in this manner, and frequently, in later days, but, at that first encounter, he felt a blend of confusion, discomfort, trepidation and detestation at the sight of a crone with hard, penetrating eyes and pinched mouth seemingly wishing to make him vanish.

Having delivered her silent belligerence, she pushed open the inner door, stopped in front of the apartment mailboxes, opened hers and, finding nothing, muttered irritably, presumably at the postman for having the temerity not to bring her mail, pushed open the outer door and hurriedly clanked the cart down the few steps on to the sidewalk and disappeared from Faisal's view. Faisal scurried back into his studio to collect his thoughts and reflect on the encounter. Once he had regained control over his jumbled brain, he began to wonder what she was doing in that apartment building in the first place. Her letterbox revealed that she was a resident. But that building was meant for students of Boston University. She could not be a student now, could she? For all the idiosyncrasies in American life he had heard about and, indeed, had briefly experienced, Faisal could not bring himself around to thinking that that bag lady was a fellow-student of his. No way. She was wearing an ankle-length gown of faded print material and whatever style, a pair of leather sandals whose better days were far behind them and, well, plainly did not *look* like a student.

Carol Whitehead. That was her name. Faisal went to check it on the mailbox he had remembered seeing the crone open. There were seven mailboxes for the occupants of that building, two each on three floors and one in the basement. She lived on the first floor. Curiosity drove him up the stairs to Apartment 2-R. He stood for a while, secure in the knowledge that its occupant had gone out, and began a wild conjecture about her and her life inside that closed door. Beyond exercising a fertile imagination, he resolved nothing. He determined to find out how she came to be living in a student apartment.

And then he found out. Not immediately. In fact, it took him almost two months, and a few more encounters with the object of his curiosity, before he got the story. Those chance meetings were surreal, at least for him, and always unpleasant. They took place in the little hallway, in the even smaller space between the outer and inner doors of the building entrance and, very rarely, on the sidewalk along Beacon Street. And she would invariably be dressed in bizarre fashion and have a headgear on. Her head would be almost entirely covered by colourful silk (or its synthetic substitute) scarves or contraptions made of transparent plastic that carried tiny pink or blue floral patterns. Sometimes she wore glasses set in a thin treacle-coloured plastic frame. Then she looked almost dignified. Once or twice, though, he detected iridescent blue eye shadows smearing the wrinkled bags around her eyes. Then she looked like a tart long gone to seed. And, without fail, she would be pushing the cart in front of her. He could not recall ever having seen it hold anything. Maybe it was because he never met her coming in from an errand.

Faisal was less uncomfortable running into Carol outside. Then he was in a crowd where he was not forced into proximity with her, and he could cast quick glances to actually look at her and the cart. Somehow she did not appear as formidable as when the encounters were one-on-one in the confines of the vestibule. Those meetings drove him into a strange paranoia. Coincidence made them run into each other a few times in front of the row of mailboxes. Since that row was attached to the outside of his inner studio wall, he could hear the vibration of it being opened by the mail carrier at around nine in the morning. He would rush out as soon as the uniformed person had gone and go for the pleasure of opening his box, expecting to find letters from home. The odd thing was that Carol Whitehead was there almost simultaneously, and he resorted to conjecture about that happening. She lived on the upper floor, and in the rear studio, and, so, unless she lay in wait at the bottom of the stairs, there was no way she could achieve her target. Unless she was a witch. She certainly behaved like one. Once or twice she glared at him for having the audacity to be simultaneously present in front of the letterboxes. She would open her box, retrieve her mail with a clawed hand, lock it with vehemence and walk past him, with the glare intensified and muttering something obviously baleful at him under her breath.

And that was the odd thing. Faisal went out of his way to be pleasant to the old woman. His tradition dictated that he should be courteous and considerate to the elderly. Then, he was a bit intimidated by the frail-looking little old woman. So he always allowed her to have first go at her letterbox while he waited patiently and deferentially for his turn. But somehow she seemed to resent him watching her getting her mail. And so malevolent stares and muttered vituperations followed. He felt hurt. Faisal then resorted to looking through the spyglass of his door once he heard the mail carrier's fading steps to ascertain that Carol retreated to her dungeon (as he imagined her studio to have been) with her mail. But he could not successfully carry out that subterfuge six days a week. And, therefore, he inevitably ran into her once or twice a week, experiencing the same attitude from her. He also developed a distinctly uncomfortable feeling that the woman was aware of the effect she created on him and doubled her malignancy to make him squirm inwardly even more.

Then unexpectedly he found out a few things about Carol Whitehead. Faisal would often use the rear entrance door of the building. And he would notice the large number of fat pigeons that hovered around, walked about or made their way in and out of a space on the first floor where they apparently made their home. And left their droppings strewn all around the rear entrance. One of the caretakers employed by the university, a grizzled stocky man closing fast on sixty, had the daily chore of sweeping away the droppings every morning from the rear outside steps. One day, as Faisal made his way out through the back door, he was leaning over his broom handle and looking amused. He certainly sounded that way as he greeted the Pakistani and remarked:

"She's crazy!"

"Who?"

"The old woman up there."

And Faisal got his story. The immediate tale was that Carol had created a lot of disturbance that morning. Those pigeons actually lived inside her apartment. She fed them, let them in and out, and took care of them. She threw breadcrumbs and birdseed out through her rear window each morning and afternoon, and the birds grew fat on them. They dutifully left behind the by-products of their digestion for the caretaker to clean up. But the old woman also fed the birds inside her apartment. And that brought in the mice. In plentiful numbers. The occupant of the apartment across from her, a law student, had complained about those little creatures, some of which had made their way into her studio. And she loathed those pests. Carol had two visitors from the maintenance department earlier that morning who almost choked from revulsion on entering the room. Other occupants of the apartment across, indeed of those above, had regularly complained of mice. Come to think of it, Faisal had actually seen one scampering across the hallway and had wondered where it had come from. Maintenance men had regularly confronted Carol with the complaints, as the current two did then. The apartment reeked of filth and squalour, and birdseed and droppings were everywhere. Cockroaches infested the place and a mice or two poked out their inquisitive heads at the two intruders.

The woman was told to clean up, as she had been told so many times before, and warned that she would be evicted if she failed to do so, as she had been warned so many previous times. And she had reacted as she had done those other times by chewing out the maintenance people for harassing her, an old woman who only cared for the birds. That morning she had also stormed to the door across from her, and, when the young woman showed her face, heaped a load of colourful invectives on her for being a snitch. The future lawyer answered back but, after a while, simply gave up and slammed the door shut.

Then Faisal got to know bits of Carol's life. For as long as the caretaker could remember, she had been living there. That was then going on some quarter of a century. She was in her early fifties then, and attractive. The birds came later, over the years, as she aged and became alone. Then she had had visitors, mostly men, but they gradually vanished and none replaced them. She also lost her neighbours of many years. When Boston University had bought the apartment complexes, the city government had stipulated that at least one original tenant in each building would stay on unless that person left of his or her own accord. Carol stayed on. And each year she had an assortment of graduate students, who never bothered to socialize with her, or, indeed, she with them, who hardly ever stayed for more than two years, but who were curious about their unusual neighbour. She would keep to herself, resent the other tenants and push her cart along the street for a couple of blocks. The university authorities had been vainly trying for the last ten years to persuade her to move to an old people's home where she would be well taken care of. They could, as a bonus, earn rent money as well. For Carol Whitehead did not pay any rent. That was one of the perquisites she gained from Boston University's agreement with the city authorities. The school even offered to pay all her costs at the home. It wanted to get rid of a bothersome pain in the neck who was giving Boston University housing a stinking name. But the old lady refused to go. She refused to uproot herself.

The fall season went into hibernation for a year, and winter made its bitterly cold appearance in Boston. Faisal, with his body used to hot and humid weather, found its bite very sharp and hardly ventured out from the comfort of his heated apartment unless absolutely necessary. Time would help his body adapt to the freezing temperature. So his Pakistani friends there told him. School was on Thanksgiving holidays and he was enjoying the few days of suspended pressure of studies. God, graduate studies in the States were so God damn tough! He was going to spend the special day, when Americans offered thanks for being able to become Americans by eating a lot of turkey and accessories and watching American football, by getting together with a bunch of Pakistani graduate students, eating a variety of Pakistani food, listening to Pakistani songs and watching Indian movies in videocassette. The day before that big day, Faisal witnessed Carol in front of the letterbox row, talking to herself and cackling, but obviously very happy. She was holding a bunch of coloured envelopes, apparently Thanksgiving greeting cards, and even threw a friendly smile at him. Faisal was surprised. The old bag lady was not without any friend or family after all! As the cliché goes, life was full of surprises.

Next year arrived and brought a cute Spanish graduate student to Faisal's building. Anna Barros was starting in the Summer session and had taken up tenancy in the apartment recently vacated by the law student. He liked her and wanted to get her interested in him. He went through the motions of attracting her attention and she responded, though not quite in the way he had hoped. She finessed her way out of his romantic overtures, but engaged in innocent flirtations and held out a firm hand of warm friendship. That was good enough for the Pakistani, starved of female company, and he grabbed every opportunity, and they were not many, of spending time with her. Besides, he harboured long-term hopes of getting her.

Thanksgiving arrived a second time around for Faisal. School went in recess and the two foreign students found more time to keep each other company. That year he cooked a Pakistani feast and invited her over to share it. While they were in the middle of the meal and were running out of topics of conversation, she remarked:

"That poor woman!"
"Why, what happened?"
"She's so alone."
"She gets a lot of greeting cards."
"She mails them to herself!"
"Nonsense! How do you know?"
"I saw her mailing them. In fact, I saw her buying those cards."

Anna related the amazing story. She had been in the supermarket when she noticed Carol buying a whole bunch of cards with different coloured envelopes. A week later, a few days before Thanksgiving, she watched her gleefully shoving those envelopes into the blue mailbox a couple of hundred yards down the road from their apartment. Anna was passing by when she was forced to wait for the signal light to allow her to cross the road. The mailbox was anchored right next to her, and Carol and the inevitable cart were parked in front of it. The cards were piled inside the cart.

"How do you know she mailed them to herself?"
"I saw the address on the top two envelopes. It's so sad."

So the old woman was a truly lonely woman, after all. That night, as he lay on his bed staring up at the white ceiling and sleep would not come to him, his mind closed in on an image of Carol Whitehead mailing holiday cards to herself and believing that she had received greetings and remembrances from friends and relatives, and then drifted off to a Carol Whitehead of a long time ago, in her twenties, and beautiful and seductive and the focus of endless male attention. She came from a respectable middle-class Boston family and worked her magic on a succession of men, breaking the hearts of a number of them along the way, and ending up in the Big Apple. She continued to work her charm but the returns started to diminish with her advancing years. But how well she lived those years. The best that New York had to offer was hers, often for the asking, and she asked frequently and for a lot, and the years passed in a flash of pleasant dreams that were only too real.

And then she was in her mid-forties. She had found time for a brief marriage where mutual jealousy negated any chance for a lasting relationship, and infidelity on both sides ensured an acrimonious divorce. She suffered through a miscarriage and three abortions and the years of riotous living eventually caught up with her state of being. The unmistakable work of time showed on her face and those charms started to fade. She was reduced to becoming the mistress of a string of sleazy men, each time coming down a notch from the lofty heights of her years of eternal spring. And then winter came with a finality that sent Carol Whitehead, in her early fifties, scurrying back to the familiarity of Boston of her early years. But the city had changed over the past twenty-five years, and she found herself friendless and forgotten in Boston. So she ended up in the Beacon Street apartment, lived on dole, and turned ancient and cantankerous and sent greeting cards to herself.

1994 arrived, but Faisal made no headway with Anna. He eventually gave up on, and diminished his contact with, her. She was going to graduate in May with a one-year M.A. degree in International Relations and was going back to Spain to pursue a career as a journalist. He still ran into Carol, still had not exchanged a single word with her, but was no longer apprehensive of her. Instead, he felt pity towards her, at her present situation and the past he had conjured up for her. He thought of his mother back home, in her late sixties, and was thankful that extended family members and friends surrounded her. But Carol only had her pigeons and mice to keep her company. And a periodic bunch of letters and greeting cards that she pretended made her loved and remembered. The pigeons visibly flourished, but, just as perceptibly, she was getting weaker.

Faisal received his MBA degree, but stayed on to try to get a good job and a green card. Summer was in full swing when one morning, while he was relaxing in bed, too lazy to get up and prepare breakfast, he heard a muffled commotion and the outer and inner entrance doors opening and closing several times in quick succession. He thought little of it and returned to his reverie. A couple of pigeons were cooing outside his window and their sounds had a soothing effect on him, accentuating the mood he was in. His parents' and his siblings' faces shimmered in front of him and they were happy and smiling. He smiled back. He was going to write long letters to them that afternoon.

He heard the news next afternoon. He was friendly with the maintenance people and, while he was sitting on the steps outside, watching the crowd with shorts-wearing young women pass by, one of them came up to him with a grin on his face:

"We're finally rid of the old woman!"

Carol Whitehead had moved out of the apartment building, or, more accurately, had had no choice but to do so. And Boston University could clean up the filthy studio, refit it and rent it out to an incoming graduate student. The caretakers had instructions from the housing department to keep an eye out for the old lady, to act in case anything went wrong with her. Knowing her disposition, they were also careful not to make their concern obvious. So they would look every day for her and her cart out on the street and, as long as they saw them, would be reassured about her well-being. They used the opportunities provided by the complainants to check in on her. And, if they did not see her for three days at a stretch, they would knock on her door to inquire if everything was all right. Most of the time there was no cause for concern, and they received an earful for their troubles. A few times they found her ill and arranged for medical attention.

The previous morning one of the caretakers had gone to check in on her. None of them had seen Carol for the last two days and that was enough cause to have a look-in. The caretaker knocked several times, but, getting no response, decided to use his master key to get in. He was greeted with the usual foul stench, cockroaches and mice scurrying to hide and a number of pigeons wandering around on the threadbare carpet of indeterminate colour and long vintage. He took in all of this in a few seconds and then his eyes rested on the bed. Carol Whitehead was lying on it on her back and looked quite dead. Only, on closer examination, she was not, but very unconscious. The doctor was called in, diagnosed her as suffering from a combination of advancing years and malnutrition, and recommended that she be permanently removed to a nursing home. Her immediate need, however, was hospitalization. Faisal guessed at the cause of the muffled sounds he had heard the previous morning.

The old lady had let loose a stream of oaths at the assortment of people around her hospital bed. She was conscious and had been informed about the decision to place her at a home. But it was a nice place where she would be well cared for and did not have to worry about meeting the costs. Her current hospital bill and the nursing home costs would be picked up by Boston University. She pleaded in vain to be allowed to go back to her apartment. That was her home. She had to look after the pigeons. She need not worry about that. The caretakers would feed them. But where would they sleep? That, too, would be taken care of. She should be thinking of herself. As she was being led away to her new home, she made one final request to the people around her:

"Ask them to look after my birds."

The 1994 Fall semester was imminent. A new tenant had arrived to occupy the rear first floor apartment of the building that Faisal lived in. A graduate student in engineering had taken over a completely overhauled fresh-smelling studio. The Pakistani was going to leave his at the end of September. He had found a good job with a multinational bank in New York and was going to move to a spacious one-bedroom apartment in a nice neighbourhood in the Big Apple. The bank was going to arrange for his green card. He was looking forward to his move, but he was also a little sad at having to leave Beantown. He often thought about Carol Whitehead. She was at the home, but the old spirit had gone out of her. The caretakers took turns to visit her once a week.

Before he left, Faisal walked around the streets of Boston a lot. He was going to come back for visits whenever he could. There was a magnetism about the old city that not all the glitz of New York could match. He often took the back door out of the apartment building. One morning, during his last week, he noticed something odd. He was leaving through the back door. The sun was mellowing in the waning days of summer. It cast a pleasing warmth around Faisal. But he did not notice that. He became aware of an unnatural silence around him. Maybe he was too preoccupied to have noticed the gradual buildup of silence over the last few days. But that morning he was struck by the complete absence of the cooing of pigeons. Their constant melody had been such an integral part of the space behind the row of buildings that they had been taken for granted and unconsciously ignored. Now that those sounds were gone, Faisal noticed their absence. He looked around. Again and again. There was no sign of a single pigeon anywhere in the vicinity. The birds had simply vanished.

Sajeda

Sajeda Rahman lay in post-coital bliss next to Eric Snow. That was their first union and the forerunner of several that late afternoon, and, after she had persuaded him to stay on and share a dinner she had cooked, most of the night as well. Both were insatiable in their physical need for each other, and the fact that it was an exotic encounter for each of them added an extra bit of spice to their experience. "It was spicier than the spicy food she cooked," Eric wryly ruminated to himself. She was a real multiple-angled windfall and, he had to admit to himself, she was terrific in bed. He felt smug. Sajeda felt a lightness of heart and a tremendous release. Almost nine years of self-imposed sex starvation for a lusty woman ended in an explosion — in a series of explosions — of shuddering ecstasy. As she idled on the bed in between urgent, intense spells of lovemaking, she dwelt on the marvel of virility that was Eric. And she felt that she could easily fall in love with him. She wondered if she had not already. Or, at least, if she was not feeling the beginning of a deep emotional attachment. She would let time sort that out. At the moment she had going through her mind the raga-based music she loved so much.

Sajeda Rahman was from Bangladesh and had been staying in the United States in several capacities for close to nine years. A government economic planning official in her country, she had availed of an opportunity of a scholarship offered by an American funding agency to study for an MA degree in Economics at Northeastern University in Boston. In January 1987, she had joined the Spring semester. Problems in getting official study leave had forced her to miss the Fall session which would have been much more beneficial in easing a Third World student into the unfamiliarity and rigours of American graduate education. When she first received the news of her scholarship and placement she was excited about the prospect of visiting the land of many Bangladeshis' dreams and hopes. Then, as her departure neared, degrees of uncertainty gripped her as she contemplated taking the quantum leap from a familiar slow-paced and poverty-ridden society to one that was fast moving, rich and, above all, alien. Then, her husband would not accompany her though her nine-year old son would. The former could have been her support in facing the new, the latter would be a comfort against loneliness, but also an added responsibility to be singly taken care of. Circumstances forced the husband to stay behind. He was also a government official. He was not provided with spousal financial aid, and did not have the means to raise it himself. Neither could he hope to obtain official leave for the two years that his wife would be away. He was that rarity in Bangladeshi officialdom — an honest person who did not live beyond his legitimate means. And so, after a night of intense lovemaking to make up for the expected desert of physical intimacy for two years, he bid his wife and son goodbye at the airport.

So Sajeda arrived at Logan Airport. Uneasiness and trepidation made her actions hesitant and shy; only the knowledge that someone from Northeastern's International Student Office and a distant relative would be there to greet her kept alive a feeble flame of courage. She had a scare when she saw out of her window her airplane landing on the runway that was literally built into the ocean. She gripped hard on her seat arms and silently prayed for a safe touch-down. The Northeastern representative, an Indian graduate student, was there. So was the distant relative with her husband and a young daughter. Only that, in a distant land, distant relatives become very close. Particularly, in the case of Bangladeshis. Sajeda was first relieved, then grateful, then delighted to see them. In a moment all her fear and nervousness vanished as she engaged in a rush of conversation with them. The Indian touch was very thoughtful of the university authorities, she reflected to herself.

So began Sajeda's brief stay in Boston that, year by year, lost its character of brevity and started taking on aspects of permanency. That initial year was hard, though. Having to get over the culture shock and adjust to the lifestyle was trying enough. Having to look after and bring up a child and grind through her university courses added to the burden. Then there was housework and social interaction with the expatriate Bangladeshi community. This group was both a necessity and a hindrance to her. They sustained her needs through frequent visits and guided her through the intricacies of expatriate life and the bargains that Bangladeshis have long learned to master — the basement sales, the constant lookout for low-priced items, in short, any means that would contribute to savings. Sajeda was grateful for their company and their concern. But she also found their company and their concern an irritation when their company hindered her studies, her housework and her solitude, and when their concern often drifted towards malicious gossip-mongering against other expatriates.

Not that she did not indulge in this behaviour, too. Most Bangladeshis, in varying degrees, do. And, in the closeness of their small expatriate communities, where they turn fiercely insular, the degree gains in intensity. Sajeda inevitably was informed of rumours circulating in the community about her. Rumours in general, coming out of the Bangladeshis' never-ending production factories, are always a concoction of a few truths, some half-truths and a whole lot of total figments of sick imaginations. Sajeda was aware that her concerned visitors lingered on to engage in gossip that inevitably boomeranged against her. She did not have the heart to ask them to cut short their visits because she also knew that realistically she could not live in isolation from them. They needed each other, including their generosity and meanness, to exist in their island of transplanted Bangladesh in the ocean of Western modernity that is the United States.

Nevertheless, that first year was trying. She missed her husband, her friends, colleagues and relatives back home. And she was nostalgic for her familiar surroundings — the easygoing lifestyle, the servants who help make it easy, the lush greenery, yes, even the polluted, dirty, congested, overcrowded nightmare that is the capital city, Dhaka. She even yearned for rickshaw rides even though they meant unstable seats, constant threats of accidents, long delays on the roads and flying dirt and noxious emission from petrol-driven three- and four-wheeled vehicles. Only occasionally, however, did she miss sex. Most nights she was simply too tired to even think about it. The solace of having her son, Tushar, with her and looking after his education and growing up kept her going. Tushar was his nickname, a phenomenon common to Bangladeshis. His official name was Naveed. He was a child not overly given to indulging in antics, and intelligent. His parents expected him to become an engineer or a doctor, and his mother expended extra care towards his formative studies. And *she* studied, extra hard, to cope with the initial difficulties of an alien educational system. Sajeda ended her first year with reasonably good grades. And she started dreaming of, and planning for, bigger things. For herself, for her son, for her husband.

Sajeda's performance gave her confidence that she could do well in the graduate education system, that, in fact, she could do even better in her second and final year that would open up the possibility of enrolling in a Ph.D. programme. A Ph.D., particularly one conferred by an American university, was a big thing back home. It would raise her status in a status- and class-conscious society, and would open up opportunities in the employment market should she look to leave her government job. Now, if she could get into a Ph.D. programme, it would mean at least an extra three-year stay after her Master's. Which would entail having to find adequate funds for herself, her son, and her husband. Of course, her husband had to come over. She, or her son, could not possibly stay away from him for a further three — maybe more — years. He could get into a graduate programme in Boston. But that could be planned for when he actually arrived. She had to plan for her own immediate future. She would apply for an extension of study leave from her government. Sajeda was confident that the approval would be forthcoming, but, if it did not, she would simply stay back to complete her Ph.D. and let things take their own course back home. She would, naturally, have to apply to extend her Master's into a Ph.D. programme and to get financial support from the university. Her current scholarship package would be discontinued at the end of two years.

Her academic success in the face of hardship boosted her overall confidence level. Consequently, she reduced her interaction with her concerned expatriate friends and acquaintances. She was now adept at hunting for bargain-basement sales and could do all the other things that they did as manifestations of the expatriate Bangladeshi sub-culture. Then she changed her hairstyle. She cut her hair short in the Western style. That induced some reaction. Her Bangladeshi acquaintances generally approved, but she was surprised when some of her American friends lamented the loss of her waist-length jet-black hair. She smiled as she thought about cultural perspectives and that the grass always looked greener on the other side. And she started wearing skirts and slacks, but that did not draw as much comment. The American friends complimented her on wearing more practical apparel, said that she looked good in them, but hoped they would get to see her once in a while in the enchanting saree. They did. But she felt more assured in going to classes, the supermarket and shopping malls in skirts or slacks bought at bargain sales. And she got herself a part-time job at the university library. She had to obtain permission from the International Student Office, but she got it almost as a formality. She was thinking ahead to the time when she would need the extra money to pay for her Ph.D. studies and the living expenses for her son and husband until he, too, could get a part-time job. But she expected some financial aid like most Ph.D. students of her department received. She increased the volume and intensity of her studies. She *had* to get into the Ph.D. programme.

And she did. Sajeda's hard work paid off. She was also given a teaching assistantship for a period of three years by which time she was expected to complete her Ph.D. She succeeded in that, too, and within the time span she was fiscally allotted. She chose her dissertation topic well, where she addressed the current trend in economics. Sajeda had finally decided on making a career in teaching in the States. There was to be no lasting return home for her. She planned on making her country of visitation the station of her permanent residency. She had grown to like it for the economic opportunity it offered, and the chance for her son to get educated and settle down in an environment he was already feeling at home in. She saw an escape for herself from the social restrictions in Bangladesh — something she had become critically cognizant of after her experience in the States. Once she discovered the shortcomings in her culture she recalled all the real and perceived persecutions she had faced from her own family, her husband's family, her husband, neighbours, colleagues — the list was long and male-heavy. Since she would find it impossible to go back and change that society in her acquired image, she decided to luxuriate in the one that had opened her eyes to its values.

Sajeda's husband never made it to the States. As the months passed neither Sajeda nor he felt it imperative for him to join her. He did not feel any urgency to escape from his impoverished tradition-bound country. He did not care for the poverty, but found many of the traditions comforting. And he was not a little frightened by what he had read and heard about aspects of American society. There seemed to be discrepancies in what America preached and what it practised. Even though he was judging from thousands of miles away and was assessing matters on the basis of hearsay and literature, it seemed to him that in some ways that society was more regimented than his. He felt no desire to settle in it. He could visit the country, purchase its products to bring back home, go for higher studies, have his son educated there, even have him settle there, but he refused to become an alien in an alien environment. He had banked on his wife coming back after two years, but there she went and got herself admitted to the Ph.D. programme. And she expected him to take a leave of three years from his job — which he was certain would not be forthcoming — and essentially be a househusband there. That he was not willing to be. Sure she wrote to him about his enrolling in a graduate programme, but since he had just turned forty and had parted ways from a mediocre scholastic life a decade and a half ago, he felt no urge to renew acquaintance with it. He had no great desire to work as a part-time clerk in a grocery store either. He felt secure in his respectable job and familiar surroundings. He would wait a further three years for his wife to come back.

But as her husband entrenched himself in Bangladesh, Sajeda did everything possible to realize her dream in the States. And, in the process, slowly, but surely, began to lose interest in her husband. She had worked so hard to make it possible for him to come and join his family. She was disgusted at his lack of an adventurous spirit, even more at his wanting to spend his life in the backwardness of Bangladesh. She was working part-time at the library, and some nights and during the weekends at a grocery supermarket to augment her earnings. She scrimped and saved, reduced making expensive overseas calls to him and, instead, wrote to him more, all the while writing her dissertation, taking care of household chores and her growing son, only so that he could come join him and better all of their lives together. That pusillanimous, unambitious, lazy idiot! Her letters to him started getting spaced out over longer periods. Oddly, so did his to her. One day, a couple of years after she had obtained her Ph.D. and had landed a job as an assistant professor in a small New England college, she admitted to herself that her marriage was damaged beyond repair. There was no hope of salvaging it, but neither did she send up a prayer for its rescue. By then she was thirty-eight, her son was sixteen and they had been in the United States for seven years.

Sajeda was attractive at thirty-eight. In fact, she looked better than she had at thirty-one. Seven years of hard toil had failed to reduce her to the state of Matilda Loisel after her ten years of slaving to pay for a lost necklace of paste diamonds. Her dark brown skin tone masked the signs of aging very well. Unless one looked closely or stared rudely, one could not discern the fine lines that subtly broke the smooth surface of her pretty face. A clever use of an array of accessories succeeded in keeping her looking soft and supple and young. Sajeda was at best pretty with large soft black eyes beneath rather straight eyebrows set fairly close to each other. Her small upturned nose was a bit bulbous at its tip and perched precariously above the space separating it from a pair of wide, full lips. She always had a pair of small earrings delicately dangling from the tiny lobes of her small ears. Her face was squarish, with a hint of fat around the fragile-looking jawbones, and her hair, now cut short, was a luxuriant silky jet-black and gently wavy. That face, without its owner deliberately wishing to, somehow succeeded in alternatively projecting the naïve and the siren. But she was perfectly aware of the baffling, occasionally overwhelming, effect it had on men. A pair of medium-sized breasts, beginning to yield to gravity but proudly held up by perfectly-fitting bras, and a narrow waist accentuating nicely-rounded hips and slim legs heightened the air of sexuality that unmistakably hung about her.

Sajeda did not give in to her powerful sexual impulses for nine years, even after she was absolutely certain that her marriage was over. Not that she was not tempted. There were the ubiquitous Bangladeshis of various ages, married and unmarried, who tried their luck in bedding the attractive single fellow-countrywoman and failed in the face of sometimes contemptuous, sometimes bored, sometimes scoffing, sometimes finessing, and, rarely, wistful, rejection. There were others, of different nationalities, who wanted to experience an exotic female, but, for the most part, she was not interested in enriching their experience. There were exceptions. There was a Lebanese in her class, as she was nearing completion of her second year of study, but, thinking of her faraway husband, she pulled back from taking the plunge. Later, she fancied a Swedish graduate student she met at work in the library and went out with him a few times, but she lacked the courage to take that important long stride to assuage her urge, even though, by then, her faraway husband was a distant unwanted memory. Returning home in the evenings to take care of her son became the crutch to excuse herself. Then she thought she would like to get close to a studious-looking young assistant professor in her department, but she could only establish a platonic relationship with him. Thus did Sajeda have her unsatiated sexual desires build up inside her, and she probably found an outlet for her frustrations in her frenzied pace of work both at her studies and the part-time jobs, her zealous attention towards bringing up her son and, later, her relentless pursuit of a divorce and a green card. And she found success.

After five years in the United States, she had a lawyer send divorce papers to her husband. She was happy, but also a tiny bit pained, that he did not contest the divorce. He must have been having flings himself, she thought sourly, and maybe he had lined up someone to marry. She also, at about the same time, obtained the much cherished, but fairly elusive, green card. A clever lawyer, a sympathetic employer who then insisted on having her part-time job turn into a full-time one, and some legal and borderline legal legerdemain worked the magic for her. A grateful Sajeda, now anointed with a Ph.D. degree, worked full-time for two years at her sponsor's supermarket store. At the end of which she found the assistant professor's job at the small New England college.

And met Eric Snow. Not immediately. Not, in fact, for two years. Those were spent in teaching, getting a few reworked chapters from her dissertation published in second-tier economic journals in the United States, and carrying out preliminary research for another article that she intended for publication in a top-rate journal. She could only exploit her dissertation so far. And she had to publish in order to obtain a tenure-track position. At the end of her first two years of teaching, she was forty barely looking thirty. And, for the first time in her life, Sajeda was all alone. Her son had left his mother's shelter. And left her empty. He had done well enough to be awarded a scholarship to study at Stanford and had left early to acclimatize himself to the California culture before classes began. He had left that evening, and that night, in the silent emptiness of her two-bedroom apartment, she let tears stream down her cheeks for a long time. That made her feel light, but no less hollow. For nine years she had taken for granted the presence and companionship of her son. He had made it so much easier for her to decide on parting from her marriage and to cope with the aftermath. And now he had turned eighteen and gone to meet a wider world. Eighteen! Where had all the years gone?

Sajeda was all alone. And all alone soon turned to loneliness of the body and the spirit. She had at different times felt the desire to be physical. For the first time since her divorce an intense emotional need grew rapidly inside her. She had to belong; she had to belong.... She had to be longed for; she had to be longed for... .

Sajeda noticed Eric the very first day. He compelled attention to himself without much effort. A tall athletically-built good-looking blue-eyed blond, he always seemed to be enjoying himself. A flashing killer smile displayed two rows of dazzling white even teeth and deepened the two just-visible shadowy furrows that slanted down from high cheekbones. Eric was aware of the magnetic character of his smile and flashed it often as well as judiciously. As he did at Sajeda. She could not fail to notice him if only because he was sitting right across from, and in front of, her. In class. The class she was teaching. He was a student in it. She was teaching a core course and most of the students were freshmen. Like Eric. He was eighteen and attending his first university class. He was pleased to be looking up at an attractive lady. He had feared it would be a frumpy old coot who would bore him into dozing off in class. Now he was certain of not having to embarrass himself in front of the class and the teacher. He smiled at that thought and the professor thought it was meant for her and she was pleased. He was certainly very attractive.

Sajeda, however, was not attracted towards him at first. He was just another student who happened to be very good looking and fun loving. He was also popular, especially with the girls. That was understandable. Then he started to talk to her after class and to visit her at her office. In the beginning he mostly wanted to know about the course, and, as the meetings went beyond the strictly formal stage, about her origin (he thought she had a nice accent), that country (he had not heard of Bangladesh, but would be happy to be enlightened by her), and her. He grew on Sajeda and she grew to anticipate and enjoy his visits. She discovered that he was from Cleveland, Ohio, came from a comfortable middle-class background and had no idea about a future career. But he was going to leave that for the future; at present, he was going to enjoy his college days. He was a wonderful cure for her solitude. Come to think of it, she realized with a mix of shock and pleasure, she did not miss having her son around in the apartment. She enjoyed being alone at night and ruminating, often with amusement, always with pleasure, her tete-a-tetes with Eric. He was so charming.

Exactly at what point Sajeda's affection for Eric as simply a student evolved into an emotion of greater interest she could not pinpoint. But she grew restless and waited impatiently in office for him to drop by. They went to lunch two or three times at quiet restaurants. There, once, he casually remarked that she was beautiful. She was flattered, thrilled, but rewarded him with only a sweet smile of appreciation. It did not even occur to her that she was in the most rigorous politically correct region of a political-correctness obsessed United States, that p.c. cops were on the prowl like the KGB in the historical Soviet Union that she had read about. She was only following instinct. She was falling in love with her student and had no desire to curb her instinct. She did not think about her college's code of conduct for teachers. Sajeda became very South Asian in the apparently emotion-regulated American society. She gave in completely to her raw emotional needs. Eric was getting a greater dose of the siren in her face. She was in no doubt that he correctly read her signals, but she decided to take matters in her hands. Before any of the young girls took him. Particularly because her forced-to-be-dormant physical desires were screaming to be released.

Almost a month and a half after she had first met him, Sajeda made her move. And he responded. She invited him over for lunch one Thursday afternoon. He would taste Bangladeshi food for the first time. He did and was overpowered by it. Her raging, rejuvenated 40-year-old suppressed hormones gained ecstatic release during a late afternoon's illusion of love. That afternoon stretched into days, then weeks. He lived in a dorm and they always met at her place, every day, for a month. Except for a few inevitable days, they made copious love until exhaustion compelled them to rest. She thrilled over his glorious young body; he reveled over her exotic one. For a month he spent his weekends at her place, but did not miss a chance to be there on the other days, at different hours. She gave herself to him completely. She was in love with him and told him so at every opportunity. He was happy to hear it, but made no effort to reciprocate. Her "I love you" carried the joy and longing of eternity and the never-ending tidal bore of her Bengali emotions. His "I love you" was a polite note of thanks for giving him a great time and making him feel special. She was not upset, however, at his lack of amorous interest. She felt positive that eventually he was going to come around. She was going to be patient and not push him. That way she could lose him for good. And Sajeda could not possibly endure that. He had made her life full after so many years of emptiness.

Then the Thanksgiving holidays arrived and he left for Cleveland to celebrate that particular American ritual. She bade him a sad farewell, but felt comforted that it was going to be a separation of only a few days. But the emptiness returned and his two brief calls only served to heighten her misery. Now she became aware of the bitter New England winter and the post-Fall trees with scanty, withered beggarly-looking leaves which wearily waited to become one with the ground below. Funny, that year she hardly noticed the arrival and exit of autumn or the approach of winter. It had been an unending spring with the scents and colours of beautiful flowers, twittering birds, blue skies and caressing sunshine. Then, for a few days, Shangri-La stopped in its tracks and time, for Sajeda, became a maddening slow crawl.

Her son had come home for the holidays, noticed her attitude and remarked: "Do you miss me so much?"

"Yes I do," reassured him.

"Then cheer up! I'll be back for Christmas!'

Christmas! That break of a month followed soon after Thanksgiving ended. Sajeda excused herself to go to her room. Her son's remark turned her inner turmoil into approaching panic. My God! Why didn't she think of that? That the Christmas holidays would be upon her in no time and would be of longer duration. If she could not bear to be apart from Eric for a few short days, how could she endure being away from him for a few weeks? And he could not spend time at her place. Because her son would be there. She wished he would not come home during his holidays. Surely he could spend them with friends. But would that solve the problem? She could not conceivably go to visit him at his house. But, would Eric come to her empty house to be away from his family during the season of family togetherness? Even for a few days? She thought not. He did not love her enough. Did he love her at all? She reprimanded herself. Sajeda had planned on him growing into love with her. She had no doubt that she could not be more in love with him. She loved him passionately, silently and with jealousy. What if he had found a white girl of his own age and had forgotten about her? No, that could not possibly happen. Could a Western white girl love like she, an Easterner, could? She could kiss and cuddle in public that Sajeda, with her Bangladeshi diffidence, could not, that was true, but she could not give him the kind of selfless love that she could. When a Bangladeshi woman gave, she silently screamed, she gave her all. Could a man ask for more?

Then Eric came back with a white girl of his own age. Sajeda saw her in the first class she taught after the Thanksgiving break. She saw a stranger sitting next to Eric. Where did she come from? Maybe she was sitting in to assess the quality of the course and the instructor. Students sometimes do that to plan for the following semester's courses. And the Spring semester was only a few weeks away. She was chatting with Eric before class and when it broke, and, in fact, went away with him. Sajeda was annoyed that Eric did not stay back to even say Hello to her. She was irritated at not getting a phone call the previous night when she was quite certain that he had returned to campus. But she had excused him thinking that he was probably busy with his friends as they caught up with one another and exchanged stories. Then Sajeda got a bit alarmed when she neither got a visitation nor a call the following day. She did not teach that day, but waited in her office until late afternoon in the hope of his dropping by. Other students did and left somewhat dissatisfied with the perfunctory, vague sessions. Their teacher was obviously distracted by something. She spent a restless night that did not do any favour for either her physical or mental state the next day. And that day she was going to teach Eric and his class. She looked terrible that morning and drank a lot of coffee to steady her nerves, and judiciously used a generous amount of makeup to make herself look presentable.

Eric, as usual, was sitting in front, looking as cheerful as ever and the girl was again sitting next to him. Sajeda made a close, but discreet, study of her because instinctively she knew that the young woman had taken Eric. She surmised that she was a good four inches taller than her own 5 feet 4 inches, pretty with hazel eyes and dark brown hair, a thin layer of unwanted fat in the wrong places, and a longish nose overshadowing a pair of sensuous lips. Her most arresting feature was a pair of enormous breasts that cried out to be ogled at. She must have spent a fortune on breast implants, Sajeda thought, though erroneously. And then, "Eric must have alternative pillow fetish." At the end of the class she asked him to come to her office.

Sajeda was calm and collected and was determined to have her inside torn apart in silence.

"Kerry's my girl. We split before I came here. We've made up." Which was stretching truth a lot. The two had been going out since their senior year together in high school and she had decided to work for a year before going to college. They were from the same small town and, beyond the occasional lovers' tiff, they never had a quarrel serious enough to lead even to a temporary split. Sajeda did not believe that part of the story, but kept quiet about it. She was determined to be composed. She was the teacher talking seriously to a student. But it took all her will power to do so.

"Then we're finished?" She knew it was a stupid question as soon as she asked it, and his silent shrug sealed the obvious answer with finality.

The dam burst when Sajeda went to the emptiness and seclusion of her bedroom. The same walls that silently recorded her frequent explosions of ecstasy now mutely absorbed her shrieks of agony. Why? And kept on asking it. She felt so dirty. She had given him everything of herself, but, in the end, she had only been an experiment in exotic woman and a fling. God, how stupid she had been! To have held hopes that eventually he would come around to returning her love. To have even thought that an eighteen-year old would have seen her as anything but another conquest in which to sow some of his wild oats. To have contemplated finding fullness in life in the muscular arms of a good-looking student. The walls seemed to have gained a life of their own and started to close in on her, slowly, looming larger and larger and narrowing the space between them and her until they were about to crush her into oblivion.

Her student! Oh my God, what had she done? Now the strictures in the college's code of conduct lashed at her with cruel and relentless force. What if the news of the affair came to the knowledge of the authorities? She would be finished — her career, her reputation, her standing in her own expatriate society. She became afraid of losing her place in that society to which, she knew, she had to turn to in adversity. After a long time, she became afraid of being judged by the traditions of a society she had thought she had escaped from so long ago. And what if the students of her class knew? How could she be sure that they were not already in the know? That Eric had not boasted of his bedding the professor, no less, to his friends? That, in any case, they had not seen the two together more than would be normal for them to put two and two together? She walked into every class no longer sure about anything. There were only a few classes before final examinations and the Christmas holidays. And each class was a nightmare. Everyone appeared to be leering at her, silently letting her know that they knew, that they saw through her façade of respectability. That they could report to the authorities. That they could talk to reporters of the school newspaper. Their faces would slowly undulate together and gradually blur into a gigantic featureless face that emitted a continuous howl of fiendish laughter. She would lose track of her lecture at different times, and the end of every class could not come soon enough.

Eric did not miss a single class. After a week Sajeda no longer saw Kerry accompany him to class. She speculated that she had gone back to let him concentrate on his studies. The day of the final examination arrived. Eric finished his exam, handed in his answer book and left the room. Except for any chance encounter, that would probably be the last time she would see him. She was sure that he would not take any other course that she taught or that he would drop by to her office to have a chat. Before he graduated he would probably have long forgotten about the teacher who loved him with all her heart. She graded his exam and gave him a B+. In her conscience she was clear that she was fair and impartial. But she knew that it would be a long time before she got over him.

Then Christmas holidays began and Eric must have gone back to Cleveland. Her son would be coming back to her in a day or two. He would talk about his freshman experiences in college. He would speak about a lot of things, but, she suspected, would probably not talk about any relationship, that is, if he had any in the first place. She would not ask him either. Bangladeshi mothers and sons normally are not as open about their relationships with each other as their Western counterparts. But she wanted her son with her. Sajeda waited for him to come back with a beating heart that would not stop its roaring.

Third World Exposition

The incongruity of it all starkly impressed upon Akhtar Akhond when he reflected that particular night at home on his first meeting that particular day with Wasim Malik. Akhtar was a post-graduate student in Economics at Northeastern University in Boston, U.S. He was from Bangladesh and, in so far as one can visualize a generic Bangladeshi, Akhtar would nicely fit the picture. A small, slightly built man in his early thirties, he had a dark brown complexion, large liquid black eyes, oily black hair, a somewhat sardonic mouth and a bony nose. Matchstick arms and a pigeon chest somehow gave him an appearance of a human sparrow. He was unassuming, with a ready smile, a hardworking student who was toiling away towards a Ph.D. degree.

Akhtar lived in a one-bedroomed apartment in Hemenway Street and lived quite unostentatiously because he did not possess the kind of money to live any better. Boston was not exactly the cheapest city to live in the United States. But he had no complaints about his circumstances. He had come from far worse in Bangladesh. He was the eldest son of a small trader in an outlying district where time took its own sweet time in moving forward. He had several siblings whom his father was determined to give an education to, irrespective of any allowable sacrifice to the family. The cost was in terms of them only existing while all suffered from poor nutrition, leaving them like images of living scarecrows. The trader aged without grace and grumbled about life's cruelty while his wife, in the tradition of Bangladeshi wives and mothers, suffered in silence, accepting her lot as preordained by fate.

Their children, however, did them proud, none more so than the eldest. Akhtar graduated with a first class Master's degree in Economics, having gained a high second in B.A. (Honours), from Dhaka University, and managed to land a job as a lecturer in his subject in Rajshahi University. A teaching assistantship at Northeastern University came his way, and he was on his way to Boston. Life there was hard; he had initial difficulties with the language, and, even after three years, had not completely overcome them. The pressure of studies exceeded the notion that he had formed back home. Above all, for a long time, he was overwhelmed by culture shock. Even after all the years, it did not quite leave him. The other Bangladeshis in Boston, expatriates over varying number of years and themselves not totally acclimatized to the alien environment, comforted him, and themselves in the process, during the early trying days.

Bangladeshis in Boston generally arrive with a solid educational background as they prepare to tackle studies at some of the premier institutions of learning in the United States. Other major cities there, as indeed in London and other important European cities, have an influx of blue-collar workers and comparatively less educated people mixed in with students and qualified white-collar professionals. Their diversity, however, does not prevent them from sharing a peculiar trait: they seem to seek refuge among themselves, as if gripped by a siege mentality, to the point where, in specific instances, they are hopelessly caught in the quagmire of a ghetto syndrome. Many never adjust to the Western environment, but, for so many reasons, the foremost being financial, they work in it and its fringes and die in it, often expressing the wish to be buried in the soil of the motherland they had left so long ago.

Thus did Akhtar survive through shared homesickness and commiseration of other Bangladeshis and by devoting his attention to his studies. He was on his way towards getting his Ph.D. That particular summer in his life pure serendipity landed him a job and an introduction with Wasim Malik. Lately he had been thinking of making a trip back home to see his family who could then show him off to relatives, neighbours and friends who could not boast of having someone from their household studying, or even working, in the United States. They would be suitably impressed — terrific! — and, in a way not too bad that — inwardly eaten away with jealousy. But for that to happen Akhtar had to earn some extra money. Then he could go home over the Christmas holidays. Before that he had to buy his air ticket and a whole bunch of gifts for his large family and a few relatives.

Akhtar made his way to the International Students' department and the job fell on his lap. Northeastern was participating in a Boston community development programme that included a six-week special course on university campus for fifty eighth-graders from a local public high school. Only that these students were part of the hard core of those Bostonians who were on the fringes of society or downright outside of it. They were the children of the ghetto called Roxbury, a miniature Harlem, only slightly less seedy than New York's ode to the miserable side of life. The expatriate Bangladeshis called it *Rakshashbari* — which loosely translates from Bengali as the abode of man-eating demons — and would not venture into it. Nor, generally, would other South Asian expatriates. Now Akhtar was being asked to undertake that leap into the unknown that was born out of ignorance, hearsay and prejudice. For the job entailed being a teaching assistant to those kids — from violence, Akhtar was certain of that, of violence, he feared — for a month and a half, for a decent pay. From a ghetto mentality, Akhtar reflected with irony, he was going to a real ghetto. From an illusion of safety through bunching around familiarity, he was to confront the preconceived danger of the unknown. But then, he thought, not so long ago he had flown from a large illuminated, glitzy ghetto — Dhaka, the capital of Bangladesh. And he needed to earn extra cash to afford the ticket back to its airport. What the hell, he was going to take the job. It was only a matter of 42 days — 2,520 hours — 151,200 minutes, and he would make enough for his return airfare and for all the gifts he was going to buy.

Akhtar began his countdown to the forty-two days by being introduced to the world he was soon going to be a part of. He invigilated the 200 or so candidates from whom the fifty lucky candidates were to be selected. Lucky, because they were to earn some money by working for a couple of hours after lessons in different departments of Northeastern University. Money was a big incentive for those who were being moulded into becoming good citizens. The initial experience of Akhtar at the examination hall was one of discomfort, of feeling like being in a fishbowl. He felt that he was being mentally probed, being sized up by a big bunch of teenagers who had little experience of a strange-looking brown man like himself. The feeling was unpleasant until it dawned on him that they were feeling equally awkward at being supervised by him and did not know just how to act at being normal. The upshot was a stiff, even somewhat formal, quiet examination in a mutually surreal atmosphere. And a sense of mutual relief when it ended.

Well, that was not such a hellish experience, after all. He even felt a little jaunty when he went to the Roxbury school to collect a few computers to carry back to Northeastern before classes started. He went by a van and an official of the community development programme accompanied him. Besides, it was broad daylight and he had just recently come face to face with a sizeable number of the area kids. His first impression was that of a colourfully-graffittied rundown area where equally rundown-looking people lounged about, looking a trifle ridiculous. His was demonstrably the only brown face in a sea of black ones. That is, until he noticed a few Hispanic ones and — he had to look twice to make absolutely certain — a couple of East Asian ones. What were they doing there? They seemed to be part of that community. Hardly had he started reflecting on that oddity before he found himself inside the compound of a very large building that was the school. It looked as seedy as its surroundings, tired and cynical about life. It must have seen so much human degradation that had Providence proffered it power of speech it would have turned it down and preferred to have remained mute. He heard later that it had been surrounded by pomp and grandeur during its early days some ninety years ago. He found that difficult to believe until he learnt that the area was prosperous in those days. He vowed to himself to learn the history of its decline.

And so Akhtar Akhond met Wasim Malik. He also made the acquaintance of the programme coordinator, white, the community development representative, black, his section teacher, Caitlin Finnegan, white, the other section teacher, Mrs. Moore, black, the other assistant teacher, white, and the two counselors, one white and one black. A gender-balanced group too, he noted. And an ethnically diverse one, with a Bangladeshi and a Pakistani thrown in. Wasim Malik was also a teacher, in charge of mathematics and computer skills. He had an aura of a friendly uncle and so was his deportment. A short man in his mid-forties, with thinning black hair baring patches of shiny pate, sporting a pair of bushy brows almost joined together that sat above a pair of eyeglasses framing luminous, penetrating chocolate-brown eyes that made even more prominent a generous hawk-like nose. He had a wide mouth whose chocolate-coloured lips were in between thick and thin, curled slightly upwards at the ends, giving an impression of a perpetually happy face. This was accentuated by a ready smile that displayed two rows of prominent white teeth. He really had a nice smile, the Bangladeshi observed to himself. A square-jawed light-brown face in which the jowls were beginning to puff out completed the picture of a nice, harmless and friendly man. And he was all of that too, as Akhtar discovered over the next few months. For their initial acquaintance developed into a friendship that sustained itself beyond their almost daily meetings during six weeks of working together.

Their initial meeting, though, was formal and guarded. The programme coordinator introduced her team to each other and the two South Asians exchanged polite, but brief, greetings. Those first "Hellos!" and slight nods at each other soon changed to "Assalamo-alaikums" and "Khoda Haafezes" as they eased into the traditional greetings of South Asian Muslims. Then the fact of being Bangladeshis and Pakistanis became irrelevant as each found solace and camaraderie in their religion and South Asian ethnicity while coping in an alien environment of different values and customs. Akhtar wondered about the situation. True, almost a quarter of a century had passed since a bitter war had led to the emergence of an independent Bangladesh out of Pakistan, and the lapse in time was long enough to have caused an erosion of acrimony in the minds of many Bangladeshis who had lived through it. Certainly those born in the new country and had created their own generational values found little time for their parents' brush with history. Akhtar had been eight or nine in 1971, when that war was fought, and had only vague memories of stifling days spent in fear and expectancy that projected from his parents, grown-up relatives and neighbours. His most prominent recollection was the indescribable outpouring of joy, interspersed with gunfire into space by Bengali freedom fighters, from all around him as the expression of the freedom of a nation.

Akhtar had never really felt any animosity towards Pakistanis. Just faint resentment perhaps, but that, too, in his early years, largely as a dutiful son dutifully feeling his parents' oral history and passion. That, however, faded simply because Pakistan did not occupy his thoughts. And before coming to Boston he had not met any Pakistanis either. Wasim Malik was both a curiosity and a revelation. As were the twenty-five kids in his — more accurately, Caitlin Finnegan's — class. The first time he encountered them, almost equally represented along gender lines, in the first class, early in the morning, he was faced with a gamut of emotions. Curiosity, a hint of resentment, a bit of cynicism and a shadow of a smile were all there, in varying degrees. So was hostility. Mainly from some of the precocious boys hardly even in their mid-teens. But they gave the air of more advanced years. Because, Akhtar reflected in retrospect, they had compressed almost an entire lifetime into fourteen odd years. Marking time by gradual linearity did not apply to them. He was shocked at being addressed as "Yo!" He had not had that form of salutation greet him thus far in the United States. There had to be a first time, he guessed. He knew about it, though. He watched sitcoms on the TV. But to actually have "Yo!" flung to his face was somewhat unnerving. Later, well into the programme, when he had gained acceptance from them, he was given several lessons in jive talk and even started using it with his bemused friends. But those first few days hostility, rarely expressed but always implied, made him doubt the wisdom of his decision to take on the job. "God, they look like criminals!" he told his bathroom mirror.

Their cold, sullen stares discomfited him during the initial sizing-up week. Gradually, however, their demeanour markedly improved as discipline, as much as familiarity, mellowed their attitude. No baseball caps in class, no chewing gums, proper dress code for the girls, no swearing and having to address the teachers and counselors as Mr.___ and Ms./Mrs.___ were strictly enforced, with the penalty of money being deducted from their paychecks for major infringement working wonders. So did getting to know each other better. "They're not too bad," Akhtar informed his mirror after ten days of interaction with the kids. He was, however, intrigued by the sight of Wasim Malik, in his mathematics and computer class, being totally at ease with those very same adolescents from the very first day. It did not make sense. Wasim was, or should have been, as much of an alien curiosity as he. South Asians did not have frequent interactions with blacks from anywhere. Then? He felt resentful that the kids threw unfriendly glances at him, while they were behaving like — well, like kids with the Pakistani. Akhtar so desperately wanted them to like him, wanted so much to get to know them and their mysterious life. "Oh, Mr. Ma-a-a-l-e-e-e-k!" delivered in sing-songy voices and accompanied by angelic smiles depressed him as he reflected on the polite, but perfunctory, "Hi, Mr. Akhond!" he received. There were no smiles for him and unshed tears only twisted and tormented his inner self. He felt resentful towards the Pakistani as he smiled back with "Yes, my dear, what's your problem?" and sedately moved towards the source of the call for help. Sometimes, the call was for nothing other than to have the computer teacher in close proximity. And, then, the realization gradually came to Akhtar that Wasim Malik's smiling salutation was not affected at all. He genuinely liked those kids, while he, Akhtar, tried too hard to be friendly towards them. That led to him piecing together Wasim's story.

The Pakistani was a faculty member at the Roxbury High School. He taught physics, chemistry, mathematics and computer skills to the junior and senior classes. And he stood out in that environment — not just school, but also the entire Roxbury community — as the sole South Asian.

"How long have you been teaching?"

"Eight years. Almost from the time I first came to America."

He had left Pakistan soon after graduation and gone for higher studies to England. He had taught school over there before deciding that he would swap Old England for New — just for the heck of it. He had been lucky in finding his teaching job without much of a gestation period. And the Massachusetts Education Board had placed him in Roxbury.

"Oh yes, I was a little nervous at first about going there. But I had taught black kids in England."

He thought for a while.

"But the black kids were a small minority over there. Here there was no one else. You get used to it, though."

"You do? How about the crime?"

"You know, I drive a new car to work and nothing bad has happened to it."

"You like the kids."

"Oh, you get bad ones each year. But others have graduated from college and are in good jobs…. Most of them never return here, though…. Some do."

Wasim was married with two young daughters and lived in a nice house in the comfortable town of Cambridge. He also had a real estate business that his wife looked after. He was obviously fairly well off, Akhtar decided, particularly after having been to his house for dinner. The Malik family was very hospitable and he was soon put at ease after the awkward introductory period.

"You don't need to teach. Then, why?"

"Because that's what I like best. Akhtar, they're wonderful kids if you really get to know them."

Akhtar decided that he had not looked into their hearts. He was stiff, artificial. He needed to relax. And, as he did so, they began to open up their hearts to him. And he gained interesting insights into the Roxbury sub-culture. In the first class Akhtar took great interest in the class oddity: a Vietnamese boy who, because of his race, stood out. He was quiet, in marked contrast to his more voluble and demonstrative classmates, did not mix with any of them, nor did any of them show any interest in interacting with him, and only talked, in his native tongue, during the class breaks, with the unusual student in Mrs. Moore's section: another Vietnamese boy. Curiosity drove Akhtar to discover that the two East Asians were sons of refugees who had set up home in Roxbury. That explained the two boys' presence in class and the smattering of East Asian faces that he had seen in that area. He also learnt that a big chunk of the black boys and girls were children of Jamaican immigrants. He, however, noticed that the children of the two immigrant groups almost never, at any time during the six weeks, even tried to talk to each other.

He learnt the reason when Caitlin Finnegan assigned a class essay on the topic of race. The pejoratives of prejudice fairly flew from the pens of almost all the students as they gave vent to their animosity against the blacks — from the Vietnamese, and the East Asians — from the rest of the class. He was puzzled and disturbed by their beliefs and behaviour and was distressed that he could not offer any effective solution towards bringing about an understanding between the two groups. It seemed that neither was in any mood to reach any. He promised himself that he would also try to figure out the reasons for the great divide in the Roxbury sub-culture. Now he had to learn both history and current phenomenon.

Akhtar was visibly distressed over two events that broke the pattern of expectation of the programme designers. One kid, slightly older than the rest, was arrested one evening for possession of a gun while on a robbery mission gone wrong. Another, a Puerto Rican, had his parents as local newspaper items. They had been arrested for dealing in drugs. He questioned his own competence as a teacher and thought long and regretfully into the night about the Puerto Rican now with a foster family. He questioned the society that was seemingly allowing human degradation to go on. He had temporarily forgotten about society back home in Bangladesh. But Wasim Malik did not seem as perturbed.

"How can you be so calm?"
"Oh, I see it all the time in Roxbury."
"Have you become so cynical?"
"No. Just more used to it all."

Halfway through the term he brought his pride and concern to his friend. "Do you know Lakeisha tried to commit suicide? Thrice?"

Wasim Malik's "I do," deflated Akhtar who thought that he was revealing something new and felt proud in doing so. Wasim's "How do you know," however, restored his pride.

"She told me herself. And showed me a scar." He was referring to a scar of her name that Lakeisha had deeply engraved on her left wrist with a sharp penknife. A friend had fortunately found her before the lifeblood had emptied out of her. "Can't we do something for her?"

"Not much. The school psychiatrist is looking after her.... So you have finally learned to relax!"

"They're also teaching me jive talk!"

"Then you've something over me. I can't speak that talk.... Never will."

"You can. You only have to listen and learn." Akhtar felt good.

Then Akhtar felt sad. The term had come to an end and a formal graduation was planned for the last day. He had become so used to the daily English class, the computer class, his fellow teachers. But, most of all, to his young charges and Wasim Malik. He felt a mystic bond connecting them together. And now that bond was about to come to an end. Wasim Malik would go back to a larger body of students, the kids would return to other kids and he would be back to his dissertation. How boring, he thought. Lucky Wasim.

"But I won't teach these kids, you know! Not for two years at least. And we'll be in touch."

Finally, graduation day came. The kids were decently dressed — as decently as their parents' meagre means would allow and that mostly meant freshly washed and ironed clothes that were worn only for special occasions. But the transformation hit Akhtar. The change from the unkempt surly kids of the first day to the well-behaved smartly turned-out boys and girls synchronized with the metamorphosis in his own outlook. They had all received commendations from their work supervisors as being diligent, polite and efficient. He doubted if these kids were going to degenerate into a life of crime even though crime would surround them in their locale. Then they were all gone. They proudly received their certificates, ate with good appetite the repast the Northeastern authorities had arranged for them, and then went away, in the process reminding everyone that they were kids who had relinquished their temporary mantle of being adults. But they abandoned it with grace and good humour.

The place all of a sudden felt empty. The Northeastern University campus, that is. It did not look deserted, in spite of summer vacation being in full flow, because there were enough people around going about their business. A group of large young men, representatives of their university team in American football, the curiously named sport where the foot rarely makes acquaintance with the ball, trundled past Akhtar, momentarily blocking his view. But he was not looking at them. His eyes were staring straight ahead, registering nothing. The surroundings felt devoid of any life because the people who gave it life for a month and a half had gone. He could almost hear the echoes of the last goodbyes.

"Yo, Mr. A, keep cool!" His name had imperceptibly been reduced to Mr. A and he relished that, as, indeed, he did the "Yo." He held in his hand the card of appreciation they had given him with all their messages and signatures signaling their acceptance of him. He gulped back a thick lump that had formed in his throat. But it came back larger when he recalled the face of Wasim Malik as he had bid him farewell.

Did he really deserve all their affections? For he had no doubt that the kids had opened their hearts out to him. But had he to them? Really? He thought he had. No, he was certain that with this group he was at one. There, he thought. *Only* with this group. Would he have mixed so freely with blacks back home? Even if they had been "this group"? Would he have been able to leave behind the acquired prejudice of his own society? He had grown up in a society that placed the highest premium on relatively light skin colour when almost all its members sported tones of dark brown. That is a society that practises racism against itself, but complains when practised upon by whites. And it made blacks the principal targets of prejudice.

Could Akhtar have risen above an ingrained belief? He had no doubt that Wasim Malik already had. But he too came from a society that held similar a similar prejudice as his. Then? Instinct told him that he would remain a prisoner of his ingrained mindset and that he would probably never be freed from it. Was prejudice insurmountable? Then, what did he really gain from his six-week experience? Only a good amount to facilitate his journey back home? Where he would be a part of an ancient implanted genetic code. And where he would probably not even think about the implant. Until he came back to Boston, to chase the shadow of a self-doubt that would not go away.

Fitzrovia

Almost every evening, that is about five times a week, for three months, I would have my dinner at Fitzrovia. An occasional lunch, too. You can see that I spent a fair amount of time there. Especially since I used up almost two hours over each of my solitary meals. The food was good without being exceptional, except on the three or four occasions when the owner cooked it himself, but the place drew me like no other restaurant in London. Oh, yes, I did sample the other fares that the city had to offer. Because, for three months, other than the rare meal I had at home, I always ate out. And breakfast and lunch had to be had. Fitzrovia did not serve breakfast. And, as has been mentioned, it was only an occasional lunch destination. So samplings from the vast array of the fascinating variety of ethnic restaurants became a daily pastime of pleasure and interest. Some had better food, almost all had a larger menu, quite a few had intriguing character, but none held the kind of charm for me that Fitzrovia did.

I liked Wagamama, that huge Japanese fast food house of massive menu that featured gargantuan bowls of noodle soup with a vast choice of meat, fish and vegetable ingredients, and a few other Japanese dishes that were consumed at one sitting seemingly by over five hundred natives and international tourists. A line that sometimes stretched a few hundred yards out on to the street waited to become a part of the cool gastronomic set. Made me wonder if the waiters and chefs were not on some kind of high to be able to cope with the unending stream of customers that did not leave a single seat free for more than five minutes. Yet, somehow, order was conjured out of chaos. Still, even this London landmark failed to capture my heart as Fitzrovia did. For me, that restaurant was a special part of the indefinable magic that is London.

I had been in London for a month before first making acquaintance with the Italian restaurant. A severe illness brought me from Bangladesh to be hospitalized and cured at the Middlesex General Hospital, a sprawling complex near the Goodge Street tube station, a stoppage that would become a regular feature of my daily life. I decided to convalesce in London, while at the same time trying to figure out if I was tired of life. Health recovery was total at the end of four months and, yes, Johnson was right over two centuries ago and would continue to be for a long time to come.

Don't think I am independently wealthy to have been able to afford to pay for the medical costs, four months' stay and regular eating out. Plus other expenses. A business enterprise in Dhaka allowed for a comfortable living and left enough for return airfare, partial medical costs and indulging in restaurant surfing, theatre frequenting and leisurely sight seeing. Such indulgence was made possible by the money saved from not having to pay for any house rent. And that is expensive in London. A family friend kindly let me have his flat in Goodge Street. He was a Bangladeshi immigrant who had gone to study medicine and ended up a general practitioner and a restaurateur, owning an "Indian" restaurant in Euston. Almost all the "Indian" restaurants in London are Bangladeshi-owned, but eating Indian food at a Bangladeshi restaurant would probably not be an attractive proposition to the many white English connoisseurs of the richly-spiced fare that is automatically associated with South Asia's biggest country. As are snakes (although that is probably becoming hackneyed and, thus, getting used less and less), tigers (although now that the animal has been reduced to the seriously endangered list, the association, though still one of alarm, is now for saving it), and beggars and fakirs (some things remain constant). Which is why the restaurant owners submerge their less familiar ethnic identity into the more recognizable one.

The family friend had done quite well for himself, his wife and his only daughter. Besides the three-bedroom spacious apartment in Goodge Street, he owned a couple of more seedy and cramped tenement houses in Brick Lane that he rented out to recent Bangladeshi immigrants. The rent was not high, but the landlord saved by paying negligible attention to the upkeep and problems of the apartments. The tenants, newly arrived from small townships, were too scared to protest to anyone and consoled themselves by complaining to God. They were just happy to be in London's mini-Bangladesh and to have found a cheap place to live in. Anyway, the owner reasoned, they had come from much worse and should not be complaining about conditions that were a luxury compared to what they were used to. And he made money that grew steadily as, like many Bangladeshis, he squirreled away in banks for the rainy days that were certain to come.

The friend was almost ten years older than I was. Actually his wife was a close friend when we were students at Dhaka University. She got married before completing her undergraduate degree, arranged by parents having fall on their lap a prospective son-in-law who was, in order of importance, a British immigrant, a doctor, and from a reasonably good family. He added his restaurant, his own apartment, his slum apartments and his only child later on, over several years, but his in-laws must have foreseen his growing prosperity to have given their daughter away in a hasty marriage. As it turned out, my friend had a happy marriage and now had accompanied her husband to Bangladesh to arrange for their daughter's marriage. That is not an uncommon practice — immigrants' children, by birth British, grown up and educated in their homeland, on turning adults, occasionally, in case of females, even before reaching the age of eighteen, being given in marriage to spouses of their parents' land of birth. Every once in a while, both before and after marriage, they rebel, and the consequences for those involved are almost invariably painful. My friends turned more to religion as their daughter grew up and, as soon as she turned eighteen and was about to enter university life, she was offered as a prospective bride for some young man in Bangladesh. She could continue her studies after marriage, that is, if her husband had no objection, the husband would become an instant immigrant to Britain and my friends would have done their duty of continuing a linkage for their daughter that they themselves had no intention of returning to. Thus they went for a long vacation to Bangladesh and I gained a rent-free apartment. Plus, on their insistence, partial payment of my medical costs. For both I was grateful. And, as a windfall, I got Fitzrovia. Or, rather, Fitzrovia got me.

Serendipity led to its discovery. By a happy coincidence it was located in a small street close to both the Middlesex Hospital and to my borrowed Goodge Street apartment. The looming BT tower nearby overshadowed it, which also oversaw the Middlesex Hospital and everything around it and, in turn, was seen from a good distance, a towering modern landmark in old, still low-horizoned London. One afternoon, soon after my hospital discharge and almost immediate occupation of my living quarters, I was walking by what appeared to be a quaint and quiet street when Fitzrovia materialized in front of me. It was not that it was hidden around a corner or anything, but the blue signboard with the slightly ornately lettered name made me stop and take a closer look inside, from the outside. The very name, "Fitzrovia," touched off visions of a romantic land where the inhabitants lived and loved with passion and intrigue. That made me wonder about the restaurant I was standing next to. Was it a place of romance and intrigue? Or, was it going to shatter the image I had built of it on the basis of a name? There was no way of knowing until I had actually been inside. You see, the place was closed and I had to satisfy myself by looking in through the glass wall. The afternoon sun gave off enough light for me to make out a few tables surrounded by chairs with red-and-white checkered tablecloths chastefully covering the tables' nudity. As far as could be made out, the tables were set with wineglasses, cutlery and napkin, but no plates. But I could only see that part of the inside that was near to me. There was no way to tell what lay beyond in the more darkened section unless I peered closely through the glass with my face pasted onto it and that, out of my own sense of decorum, I flatly refused to do. But there was no doubt where I was going to dine later that evening.

No, the interior did not disappoint me. It was thrilling to take in the laid-back, intimate atmosphere. You felt like you were in your own small dining room, doing as you pleased. And, at Fitzrovia, as I gradually discovered, you did almost as you pleased that first shocked, then helped put at ease, newcomers to that hole-in-the-wall lounging den that masqueraded as an eating place. It adopted a minimalist décor partly because its dimensions would not allow it to do otherwise. It was tiny, with just enough room for two square wooden tables, each being surrounded by four aquamarine-coloured wooden chairs on each side, entrenched near the glass wall, and adjacent to each other. A rectangular table stood opposite them, surrounded on one side by a continuous curved dark brown leather-covered sofa and, on the other, by a few of the aquamarine wooden chairs. That table took care of another ten customers, that is, if one was not reclining on the sofa, as was not unusual. This table was the first sight as soon as one entered the restaurant since it was placed a few feet away directly from the door, also painted aquamarine. "The owner must pine for the sea" flitted through my mind the first time I went in. The seating arrangement was completed by a smaller square wooden table that was located in what I had seen as the dark side from the outside, but was really a small space close to the stairs that led down to the basement kitchen and the single toilet. This table, covered with the ubiquitous red-and-white checkered cloth, had two accompanying wooden chairs painted — you guessed it — in aquamarine.

    A maximum of twenty people could be accommodated at one sitting, and sometimes the maximum was reached. However, most times, the small table did not entertain customers but, rather, the owner and his wife, or the chef, or a visiting friend. Sometimes they ate, other times they just had a chat over a glass of wine or coffee, and, almost invariably, the owner calculated the bill on it on a small rectangular piece of whitish paper to present to the often reluctantly requesting customer. The original paintings by a well-known avant-garde artist adorned two opposite walls and very nicely complemented the ambience of the place. A small wooden semi-circular enclosure at the back, at right angle to the top of the stairs, held the cash box, bottles of wine, an assortment of wineglasses, other odds and ends, and a little TV uncertainly perched on the formica top. Quite often the TV was turned on for the owner and, if they were present, his buddies, to watch the English premier division football matches, particularly, as was often the case, if the teams contained Italian players. The diners could watch too and give loud vent to their feelings, as Giovanni and buddies often did.

Giovanni was the owner. He was Italian. He had a bit of a Sylvester Stallone look about him, especially around the mouth. He was in his early forties, just short of medium height with wavy black hair, large soulful eyes, a firm jaw from which the skin had begun to sag, and a languid manner. He spoke English with an accent that was neither thick nor thin, and with only occasionally faltering grammar and syntax. He was from the southern part of Italy, while his russet-haired, pale blue-eyed wife was from Florence. She was more businesslike and was not very well liked by the female customers. She was friendly enough with me. They had a girl aged ten, a spitting image of her mother, and a boy two years younger, closely resembling his father. They were born in London, went to school there and were very English with the exuberant Italian genes displaying themselves, more in the boy, every so often. Giovanni doted on them as he did on the black house cat which was an integral feature of Fitzrovia. And a very spoiled feature. As well as a very loved one. There was a distinct correlation between the two attitudes.

I think I have mentioned my interest in the theatre. Only interest? Try passion and you will be closer to my feelings for that particular art medium. And London could not be bettered as a conduit between my yearning and its realization. I watched a lot of plays — in the theatre district, outer London, fringe and pub theatres — and even managed to meet some of the famed and yet to be renowned performers and directors. And a happy coincidence kept me in Goodge Street. Not only was the theatre district within reasonable walking distance up Tottenham Court Road, but Gower Street was in even closer proximity. On that street is located the Academy, that is, the Royal Academy of Dramatic Art — RADA, as it is more commonly known — the institution that produces many of the actors and actresses who light up the theatre scene. Curiosity often had me pass by the old building prominently displaying a pair of sad and happy masks which were blackened with grime. Once I managed to get inside and talk with the receptionist as students flitted in and out or hung around the lobby. So, one day they were going to be out there, taking on the personalities of different characters, but, in reality, also reflecting the various emotions of the audience. Maybe some would go on to become international names. Surely, though, some would fail and gradually fade away from the scene. Then the sad mask in front of their alma mater would take on a life inside them for who knows how long. I wanted to know about these students. Fitzrovia provided the opportunity.

High summer was in glorious progress that year in the second half of the last decade of the old millennium. Summers in England, as I was told and as I subsequently discovered on two further trips, can be either very hot or cool and clammy. That year it was neither, with the weather pleasantly hot with continuous sunshine and warm blue skies decorated with fluffy white clouds. And when, on the odd days that rain fell to break the monotony of the sublime weather, it descended in a soft patter, taking care not to ruffle anyone and leaving behind a bracing freshness on everything it had touched. Summer school was in progress at RADA and most of the three-year students were on vacation. Yet, the first RADA students I encountered at Fitzrovia were two of the three-year ones. And that, too, on my very second evening at the restaurant, which was the very next day following my initial visit.

The black cat was the first host to greet me on the first day. Once I pushed the front door open and took the first hesitant step in, a polite questioning "Meeao?" from a small quizzical face with the right front paw raised a couple of inches above the wooden floor instantly put me at ease. I actually answered with a "Hello!" and was bending down to pat her (she was a she) when a male "Hello!" made me straighten up. And that is how I first met Giovanni with the lazy smile. There were no other customer, thus enabling me to have the table by the glass wall and make the owner's acquaintance. After taking my order from the small handwritten menu of two pages and a bit of another, he came and sat at my table while I was having my after-dinner cappuccino. I guess he was as curious about me as I was about his restaurant. He would often do that, sit at the table with his regular customers, sometimes during the course of the meal, more often after, and chat. Everyone seemed to be glad to have him as company. I know I was. The illusion of being at home sharing repast and small talk with an unexpectedly dropping-in friend was so naturally set up in the Fitzrovia atmosphere. And the restaurant catered to a lot of illusion makers.

The second evening the famous director walked in. He was instantly recognizable from his pictures, unless he was an identical twin or a very closely resembling double. Giovanni greeted him like an old friend and the English director reciprocated the Italian hug. The two were old friends, from the days when Fitzrovia was one of the most sought-after and chic places in London. A miniature Wagamama with a full clientele belonging to the world of dream-makers, but without any waiting line snaking out on to the sidewalk. This history of glory past I learnt later, little by little, from different sources. Some of those who had shared in that glory, indeed helped make it, still came back for old times' sake. But fewer and fewer as days went by. In those days Giovanni cooked himself and his fare and the atmosphere combined to attract his clientele. His cooking must have been sublime. He did me the honour of cooking for me a couple of times or so. In his sparse menu he had a pheasant dish listed. It was only rarely available and, whenever it was, I never failed to order it. And Giovanni cooked it and allowed me a taste of his artistry. He did not cook anymore; he hired an Italian who spoke no English to do it. And he kept Fitzrovia running only as a living monument to memories of other days when a television channel operated from just down the street, and the actors, directors, producers, writers, technicians and others involved with it made the restaurant their own ode to lunch and dinner. Then the TV station moved a long distance away, but Giovanni did not. And he became a glorified slum landlord. He bought up a number of old apartment buildings around Fitzrovia, rented them out to low income tenants, did little to halt the slow but certain descent of the apartments into decrepitude, and made enough money from them to get by in comfort.

Then I saw a couple of RADA students — the three-year ones. They were on summer vacation and two summer school programmes were going on. Soon I would be seeing and meeting the students from those courses — mostly Americans — but the two long-termers were the first I sighted. They were two males in their twenties and did not look anything out of the ordinary. They spoke with each other and with Giovanni, all very polite but relaxed, had their food and left quietly. They came back a few more times and eventually I made their acquaintance, at which point they gave me the distinct impression of being a bit neurotic. Which made me recall someone telling me that actors are spaced out and mad or they would not be in their profession. Over three months a few other three-year students made sparse appearances, telling Giovanni that they had come up to London for a day or two and thought that they would get back into an old habit. That was it — Fitzrovia was a haunt and a tradition.

Then the summer school students arrived — in large numbers — as I mentioned, mostly Americans, who tried their hardest to suppress their Americanism, but only succeeding up to a point. They were caught up in a RADA tradition that will go on as long as Fitzrovia exists and the Academy does not move a ridiculous distance away from its Gower Street location. Very soon the short-termers became familiar friends of Giovanni and the cat. The women adored the cat. And they adored Giovanni. And Giovanni adored them while keeping a nervous eye over his shoulder. His wife had the habit of dropping in at any odd time. She would greet the women with a fixed smile, get uncertain smiles in return, and call her husband at the table-for-two to discuss business. Then the atmosphere inside became uncomfortably formal and everyone seemed to be talking in undertones. When, as happened more sporadically, the children came in, they got fussed over, but they were more interested in fussing over the cat. Lucky cat!

Sondra and Paul were ever-present fixtures who adorned the place. She was American, he Canadian, both in their mid-twenties, and both were in the summer school. They met at breakfast at the RADA cafeteria and instantly hit it off. Physically they were a fine match. He was tall, angular, with a lean face featuring a head of shoulder-length, chestnut-brown straight silky hair, a pair of brilliant blue eyes underneath thin eyebrows and above a straight nose with a pronounced tip that dominated a sensitive mouth and neutralized the prominence of a sharp chin. She was of average height, with a square pretty face made lovely by a glorious head of thick cascading red hair, small ears that carried off-beat jewelry, finely arched and neatly plucked eyebrows which brought out the perkiness in large blue-green eyes, and a small nose turned just a bit upwards at the tip. She also had a wide mouth with sensuous lips that often broke into a dazzling smile of gleaming white teeth, twinkling eyes, and a smooth skin from which intermittent freckles stared back at you if only you specifically looked for them. He was from Toronto, she from California, born and brought up. He walked briskly and purposefully; she with a lazy gait that invariably forced him to slow down his pace. Both belonged to quite well to do families and wanted to be actors. Both were in endearing love with each other.

Eric and Tim were also Fitzrovia frequenters. They were Americans, Eric in his late twenties, Tim in his early thirties. They were not in love with other. Certainly Eric had no feelings other than camaraderie towards Tim, but Tim thought that he was in deep love with Eric. Deep infatuation was what he actually felt, and he pursued the object of his desire with relentless energy. But Eric had a partner waiting for him in California whose picture was prominently displayed in his dormitory room, but Tim, who had recently broken off with his, ignored the message. On finishing his RADA course, he decided to move from his native Chicago to California. I got to make their acquaintance and both appeared distraught, though for different reasons. Yet they hung out together, sometimes by themselves, more often with groups of course mates of both sexes. His family tolerated Eric's sexual orientation, Tim's made him a pariah. Eric was appreciative of his for at least recognizing a difference, Tim was resentful and defiant. For him to move to California would provide him an opportunity to move away from rejection and to move closer towards pursuing the twin dream of a profession and an infatuation.

Sondra and Paul occasionally were part of the group that hung out with Eric and Tim. Eric visibly relaxed when he was with the larger bunch, but, equally obviously, was tense and morose when one-on-one with Tim. But, nevertheless, he hung out with him. Sondra and Paul indicated that they were in love. It pleased me to see them so much into each other and told them so soon after making their acquaintance. They smiled. Then, one day, they went into a violent argument that took no notice of anyone around them. Including a foursome of manicured business executives, equally divided between the sexes, looking fiercely professional, but who were there to soak in the artsy ambience. They were startled to experience such tumult in the creative world. And were stunned into silence at the colourful words and screams that were coming from the adjacent table. But they were loud enough and articulated well enough for the rest of us to hear and understand. I was having my solitary lunch at the table-for-two with Giovanni in attendance, both of us sipping white wine. Four or five summer-termers, as well as Eric and Tim, occupied the large sitting area and had the cat for company. Giovanni was perturbed because of the disturbance to the new corporate world customers, but kept quiet, thinking that his two old reliable patrons would soon exhaust their excess energy and calm down. But they did not anytime soon and Giovanni started to get agitated. I was feeling saddened at my two friends' (I had upgraded them from the acquaintance status) possibility of breaking up. Because that is what they were threatening to do over, admittedly, some serious problems. Could they not talk it over? I and my idyllic vision of life!

Their screaming increased in intensity, the cutlery was set for some serious damage, the cat threw a glance, at once accusing and fearful, at their direction and slunk towards the stairs leading down to the kitchen, and Sondra stormed out of the door. Paul made no effort to follow and shouted to no one and everyone, "It's over!" and then pondered over whether to leave or to stay and ruminate. The manicured ones returned to a silent lunch gone cold. And Eric went out after Sondra and Tim came over to Paul. So did Giovanni. And, slowly, the Canadian calmed down. This time exhaustion gripped him and he looked like he had been drained out of water. He was given consolation and advice, but he did not look like being consoled or being amenable to listening to any advice. He soon looked distraught and full of remorse. If Sondra had come in then, he would have taken all the blame on himself and begged to make up. But she did not come in. Eric did and told Paul:

"Just give it some time."

Was time going to be the great healer then? I hoped it would.

In a sense it did. After all, close to twenty four hours had passed since Sondra had left at around eight the previous day, to her and Paul's entrance together at around six o'clock the next evening. They came in with big smiles, arms around each other's waist, looking terrific, and she gave Giovanni a big hug that he held on to for a while and made tighter. He was secure in the knowledge that his wife would not come in for at least another two hours. I was happy. The cat rubbed up against Sondra. And Fitzrovia went back to its dreamlike existence. For a few days. Until the two went into another intense argument at lunch, with Giovanni and myself as spectators. Again sadness pervaded over me because romanticism would not let go of me.

"They're not going to be together much longer," Giovanni told me.

"Why not?"

"Because there's no point."

Bloody cynic! Eat your words, Signor! They were back together within the week. Their term was also coming towards an end. Another three weeks and RADA would become a memory for them.

Eric and Tim were also coming to their last few days in London. And at Fitzrovia. So was I. I was going to head for home a couple of weeks after they did. For one thing, my flat was going to be reoccupied by its owners. For another, my financial resources were coming to their logical end. Besides, summer was coming to an end and I had no wish to face the winter in London. But I was going to come back, if not next summer, some other summer. Eric perked up as his departure neared. Tim became depressed. He, however, told me that it was because of the certainty of his having to leave London.

"You know, I don't know what it is about this place that won't let you go..... London's magic!"

They did have a tiff, those two, a few days before they left. I was not there to witness it, but Giovanni told me. Tim could contain himself no longer. He almost demanded an affair and wanted it to continue in Los Angeles. He was moving there to be near Eric. Maybe they could move in together. What did he see in the other guy anyway? He loved him. Why didn't he try to understand that? But that was calling for rationalization. Tim was crying out from the heart and that led to some heated words. There was no one else present except Giovanni and, this time, he intervened early to stop things from getting worse.

I must confess to being mystified about gay love. Yet, I accepted gays as my friends. The only thing is that I made these friends in London. I never met one in my own society. Yet, I know they are there. Other people have met them. But they choose to remain in the shadows because their society does not tolerate their deviation enough for them to flower under the sun. So they are to remain where the sunlight is blocked out. I was born in that society and have absorbed some of its strictures that I otherwise feel are outdated. So, while gays are kosher as friends, love among them is a thing of mystery. And, yet, I consider myself to be rational. There were other gays, of both sexes, in that RADA crowd — which is how I made friends with them — but they were not emotionally involved with one another, nor did I find them as fascinating as Eric and Tim. I met them together one last time the day following their course completion.

A whole group that filled up Fitzrovia came in that evening for a last fling of camaraderie, to burn forever into their heart an out-of-the-way hole-in-the-wall place where they had made time stop for a few hours evening after evening after evening. There was a lot of laughter…there were a lot of tears. There were a lot of caresses for the cat which, as if sensing the moment, did not try to escape from their essential uniformity. And there were a lot of hugs and kisses for Giovanni who was not looking over his shoulder. But his wife did not come in that evening. Then they were gone, soon to be scattered with little likelihood of being together again. Tim stayed back a few more days, to soak in London by himself and then to make a trip to Brighton, before flying off to Chicago to bid farewell to that city. He came in to Fitzrovia for the four days that he was in London, but the charm had dimmed for the both of us. It was time to leave. Tim was despondent all those four days. He never told me the real reason for his state of mind, but he did not have to. He could not go to Brighton quickly enough.

Sondra and Paul also came in that last evening. Separately. And they did not speak to each other. He came in briefly, for a perfunctory farewell to all, as he was taking an early flight next day for Toronto. Sondra was already there and the place was too small for the both of them. Giovanni was right. I was wrong. Those two were not meant to last. They had broken off a few days before the summer term mercifully came to an end for them. Neither showed up at Fitzrovia those last few days, but they could not go their separate ways without a final bow to the symbol of their days of laughter. He was not his usual smiling self that evening, but he was friendly and courteous to all. Nevertheless, Paul gave the impression that he wished his early flight next day would be brought forward that very moment. Sondra was more relaxed, smiling, but the storm she had just been buffeted by was easily discernible beneath that happy façade. Then, they, too, were gone. I strode out for my place. And Giovanni turned out the lights.

My time of departure was very near. As if enticing me to stay on for a bit longer, summer in its waning days became spring-like. Unending mellow sunshine, silky nights and fragrance in the air were compelling sirens. But my devilishly unswayable mind reminded me that they would be ephemeral and worth ignoring. Besides, there were other mundane reasons to leave. Sometimes one has to just pack up and leave. Such, indeed, is life. Then it was time for my last evening at Fitzrovia. Giovanni cooked for me. There was no pheasant, but the art of fine Italian cooking was there in all the dishes. He came with a glass of white wine and sat at my table for a while.

"Are you coming back?"

"I hope so.... I will."

"When?"

"Don't know. Maybe next year, maybe the next. You'll still be here?"

"I'll still be here."

His wife was there that evening. She had given me a smiling hug and had gone to sit by herself at the table-for-two. And every once in a while, when I chanced to look in her direction, she threw me a meaningless smile. Later that evening the three-year RADA students started coming in. Their classes would resume soon and some of them had come back early. And lost no time in making an appearance to their place of pilgrimage. They came in small numbers and the place took on an English atmosphere. Different from that of the high summer, but, nonetheless, pleasant. A few of the female students also came in, to greet the cat and hug the smiling owner. The cat for a moment hesitated and looked suspiciously at the cuddlers, then purred when memory brought back familiarity. The owner's smile was warm and welcoming, but his hugs were of very short duration and he allowed only a quick peck on the cheek. So, some of them were going to be household names of tomorrow. Or, at least get wide recognition. Plus money, honours. Then Fitzrovia would become a distant footnote on their journey towards realization of a dream. And those failing in their dream? Would they return to Fitzrovia to recall wonderful moments on the way to bitter failure? That is, if Fitzrovia was still there.

And what of the summer-termers? They also had dreams. Most would not have theirs realized. But they would still retain wonderful memories of Fitzrovia. Another two female students came in to greet, and be greeted by, the cat and the owner. Giovanni's welcome was still laced with caution. His wife was sitting by herself at the table-for-two and smiling every so often. And she kept an eye on him through her smiles, and he kept an eye half on himself and half on her through his own languid ones.

Three Women — and a Bond

Shahana Ali, Nabila Khan and Seema Chowdhury were more acquaintances than friends, although they were friendly enough to each other — for the most part. This needs a qualification. The distinction between the terms "acquaintance" and "friend" gets blurred in the psyche of the average Bangladeshi. It becomes clearer in the ethnic Bangladeshi British, but not always. Acquired convention every once in a while brings back the haze. Shahana, Nabila and Seema were young women of Bangladeshi ethnicity. Shahana and Seema were twenty-three, Nabila twenty. They had known each other for about three years without ever becoming close. Yet, other Bangladeshi expatriates called them good friends. Sometimes they would do the same when talking about the one or the other to someone else. To a Bangladeshi man, even a chance encounter followed by a meeting or two with a person entitled that man to call him a friend. The use of "him" is deliberate since very rarely will a Bangladeshi man term a woman a "friend." Instead, the reference to a woman will be along these lines: "Yes, I know her," or, "We were in the same class in the university," or, "I met her at this or that house or at this or that party." The Bangladeshi tradition is notoriously difficult to shift position, let alone significantly change, and the idea that a woman can be a "friend" is gaining ground, but at a pace that makes a turtle a world-class sprinter.

If the acquaintance is anybody important, then he becomes someone's "great friend." So does he to a social climber. Should he fall from his lofty heights, he falls hard. Then he is hardly mentioned, even as an acquaintance, by the same people who had, without his approval, claimed him as their "great friend." However, in general, the fuzzy area dividing, as well as connecting, the concepts of "acquaintance" and "friend" is unaffectedly Bangladeshi and people are happy to call each other friends even if, in Western terminology, they are acquaintances. At least in this instance, the East does not meet the West even if the East has been physically present for a long time in the West.

    Shahana and Seema spoke Sylheti, Nabila a mixture of genteel and colloquial Bengali. All spoke English like natives. Because they were natives of London. Every now and then they would slip in a London turn of phrase in the local accent that made tourists, used to listening to only BBC English, wonder if the English spoke a different language at home. Shahana and Seema were born in London of Bangladeshi immigrant parents and Nabila was of immigrant parentage too, but she was born in Dhaka and had emigrated with her parents when she was a two-year old toddler. Shahana and Seema's parents were from Sylhet, Nabila's from Dhaka. There is no difference between Sylheti and Bengali and there is a world of difference between the two.

    Sylhet is a district in northeast Bangladesh. The indigenous people there speak Sylheti, a Bengali dialect. There are several Bengali dialects, some more difficult to understand than others, spoken in different districts in Bangladesh. Yet, in Britain, Sylhetis speak Sylheti and the rest of the Bangladeshi expatriates speak Bengali. And the Sylhetis look at the rest of these expatriates as "Bangalee." The fact is that the vast majority of Bangladeshi immigrants in Britain are of Sylheti origin. They were the first big wave that went there as far back as when Bangladesh was a part of British India. And successive waves followed them, as Bangladesh became an independent country. Many of the early immigrants were menial workers, seamen, and marginal farmers — people with limited education at best — who went to the new land for a better life. They pioneered the formation of the small and large Banglatowns in London by concentrating as a group to find warmth and familiarity in each other and to collectively face up to the perils of an alien culture and society in which they were supposed to integrate. Most went through terrific struggles to establish themselves. In the end, they only succeeded in being able to live in brick structures, securing British passports and being able to afford sporadic trips to

Sylhet where they became objects of curiosity, pride and envy of their relatives and community. Plus the targets for requests for sponsorship to make them immigrants. And, thus, near and not-so-near relatives managed to augment the Sylheti population in London. And strengthened the Sylheti sub-culture there.

Other districts slowly made inroads into Britain, but collectively, they are far smaller in number than the Sylheti population and its British progeny by birth. And, collectively, they are "Bangalees" to the Sylhetis. Some jokes about each other, some resentment against each other exist, but they are neither offensive enough nor hostile enough to cause a permanent rift between the two groups. For all of them, their ethnic pride in being Bangladeshis by origin overrides all frictions at the sub-cultural level. But the British-born progeny of the Sylhetis only speak and understood Sylheti, that is, if they speak the language at all, and those of the others a commonly-understood form of Bengali, again, that is, if they elect to at all speak the language of their parents. This is a generalization; there are exceptions and some Sylheti-speakers of the second generation understand and speak general Bengali. However, they have often grown up in households where they have only heard Sylheti or general Bengali spoken and simply speak what they have heard. Often they cannot write what they speak and they are on their way to being progenitors of pure British whose ancestors had arrived from a distant land called Bangladesh.

Shahana held a Master's degree in biochemistry and had landed a reasonably well-paid job as a research scientist at a biomedical company. Her father was an educated man — he had been a high school assistant headmaster in a small town in Sylhet — and he had done well in business ventures in London. He was thirty four when he had emigrated to Britain, courtesy of marriage to an immigrant's daughter. His wife had been born in Sylhet, went to London when she was twelve, studied enough to learn conversational English, but not that much to take her O' levels and, after eight years, was taken back to her district of birth by her parents to be married to the assistant headmaster. Her father and her husband's father were from adjacent villages and were distantly related. Her parents were pleased to get an educated son-in-law and arranged for him to immigrate and look after their businesses in Brick Lane. That meant a shop that sold Bangladeshi and Indian clothing, another that carried an assortment of Bangladeshi, Indian and Pakistani sweetmeats, and a third that sold odds and ends for everyday use. Their son had helped them run the shops, but he had turned eighteen, had been admitted to a good university to study engineering and gave clear signals that he was going to turn his back on Brick Lane forever.

Hired assistants ran the day-to-day business at the shops, but the owner felt the necessity of an educated family member for peace of mind. And that is where the son-in-law came in. Of course, there was no question that he would live with his wife at his in-laws' house. There was ample space and the son would only visit on holidays until he became a qualified engineer and would only have the time and inclination to make the occasional visit. More likely, the parents would have to visit him, but that was in the future. At that moment, they were concerned with setting up their son-in-law in business and he did not disappoint. And did even better. His parents-in-law became grandparents of two girls and a boy, all in the space of five years, and he had prospered enough to buy a four-bedroomed house in Euston where he moved in with his family. He left Brick Lane, but did not abandon it.

Shahana's father opened restaurants in Charing Cross, Tottenham Court Road and Soho. These "Indian" restaurants, with better décor and superior service than most "Indian" restaurants in London, attracted a good number of tourists as well as home clientele eager to sample the exotic, or the "in-thing" in British gastronomic habit, or, simply to indulge in favourite cuisine whether it was "in" or "out." The menu, mostly Pakistani and North Indian with a few Bangladeshi dishes thrown in in the hope that they would be exotic enough to attract the curious, was good too. As he prospered, he expanded into the electronic goods business and did well. Well enough to be able to afford efficient managers to look after the Brick Lane shops. And to provide good living for his family and first-class education for the children. A sister followed Shahana. Two years younger, she had just graduated with a degree in Economics and was all set to start in an MBA programme. The son, a further three years younger, was planning on becoming a doctor. Their parents were happy — their offspring were, or were going to be, in professions deemed respectable by the Bangladeshis, expatriates and home variety alike.

Shahana lived at home with her parents and siblings. She was under stricture to return home by early evening unless she had obtained parental permission for some social occasion. In spite of her birth and upbringing away from the mores and taboos of her parents' homeland they bound her in her own country. And she submitted quite willingly to them. Not just because she was living under her parents' roof. She chose that too. Her own earnings would have enabled her to move out on her own. She was short and rather rotund without appearing ridiculous. Actually, she was very attractive. Yes, she had a face inclined to roundness, plump arms, an extra layer of fat around an otherwise narrow waist, wide hips and round thighs. But that face featured a delicate nose, soft rosy lips inviting to be kissed, small ears, and carefully-plucked arched eyebrows that perfectly complemented her most beautiful features — a pair of eyes that would be the definition of the term dreamy eyes. They looked at the world with a touch of irony from underneath long eyelashes. They suggested and provoked. The colours of the irises seemed to change from grayish to light brown to a cloudy mixture of the two. They were hypnotic and they hypnotized a lot of men. A broad forehead began a cascade of very fine silky brown hair that she let fall to her waist. She had startlingly large breasts which would inevitably, within a few years, sag and lose their haughtiness. But at the time they proudly proclaimed their thrusting presence from the twenty-three-year-old body. Shahana was buxom, but the sum of her parts made her voluptuous.' Her small, shapely hands and small bones made her look delicate without any suggestion of fragility. Then there was her skin. They looked soft and satiny. She was much lighter-toned than the average Bangladeshi and there was absolutely no blemish on any part of her skin.

Shahana had eyes for only one race of men — white. She got them all right. From the age of seventeen — when she lost her virginity to one — till six years later, she had already gone through eight. And planned on having more before she got married at around thirty — to a white man. Her parents did not know that yet; she still could not muster up the courage to tell them of her plan, but she did tell them that they should not look for a husband for her for at least another five years. She was not ready to marry; she was going to concentrate on her career. She planned on becoming the chief scientist of her company, but that would not be the limit of her ambition. She wanted to be internationally recognized in her field. Her parents put up a feeble protest, reasoning that several eligible Bangladeshi-origin young men were interested in marrying her, that some of them were to their liking, that she would not find the right kind of husband when she was near thirty, that marriage would not be a problem for her career plans, that other Bangladeshi women were managing both marriage and career. Shahana, however, stood firmly adamant on her principles and they did not press further because they feared losing her. They knew she could afford to live on her own and they liked having her around. At least they could keep an eye on her. If they suspected the real reason for her reluctance at marriage they kept their own counsel. And even if they suspected they had no solid proof to confront her.

Shahana was careful not to bring her love-life home. That would have been a disaster when she was seventeen; it would have been a disaster six years later, and in all the years in between. She was never in true love with any of the eight men she had gone to bed with, only infatuated with some, and physically attracted for a specific purpose with the rest. She was aware of her own feelings, which made it easy for her to break off the liaisons, but which left two of the men with shattered hearts and four more with bruised egos. Sometimes she wondered if she was even capable of loving, but she was not going to force herself into finding true love. But she always found ersatz and unwanted love. That did not get spread around the Bangladeshi community. She contributed to that by keeping her interactions with it to a minimum. She had stopped going to Brick Lane for a long time, since the time her aged grandparents came to live with them and, except for a very few, and those too mostly women, had no friends in the community. When relatives and family friends came to visit at their house, she did not make herself available beyond the expected courtesies. All of which made her immune to the powerful gossip machinery that operated in her community.

Her first affair she had with a classfriend's older brother in his apartment. It was easier in the university, both in terms of space and time and protection from unpleasant rumours. She went to class from her home, but there was the excuse of library and laboratory work to cover many explanations. And it was normal for university students to mingle, and Shahana was careful to keep exclusive mingling to a minimum and only for relatively short duration. And so kept out undesirable prying eyes and ears. There were other South Asians, including Bangladeshis, at the university. Once she found her job her position eased as her manoeuverability increased. Now she had no Bangladeshis as co-workers and she had to go out of town for conferences and work-related activities. The last was in Switzerland where she met an Italian tourist and she had eight nights of ecstasy out of ten days of busy business and work schedule. Sometimes she thought of the strains she put herself through to satisfy her adventurous spirit and to keep it in darkness from her parents' community, and particularly from them. Then she toyed with the idea of moving out on her own and thus avoid prying eyes and suspicious minds. But each time she abandoned it. She was too attached to her parents and siblings, of which the sister was her roommate and soulmate, the one whom she opened her heart to, who knew about her affairs and who kept the knowledge to herself.

Among Shahana's few Bangladeshi friends was Seema. They had met at a Bangladeshi wedding a few years ago. The bride and the groom were of Sylheti parenthood and a big chunk of the Sylheti community was invited to the wedding at the Whitechapel community centre. Neither Shahana's nor Seema's families were related to either the groom's or the bride's except in a remote, roundabout way that Bangladeshis are often fond of discovering, especially as expatriates, but they were educated and respectable members of the community and were invited. Shahana immediately took to the vivacious sixteen-year-old and thought she had found a soulmate in the community. She did - up to a point. Seema had the kind of face that could not be called pretty but attracted more attention than most good-looking women. However, she was not repulsive looking either. She had the normal Bangladeshi dark brown complexion. Her jawline was somewhat irregular, making one side of her face appear slightly skewed and the part of the mouth on that side drooping down slightly more than the other half. It had the effect of giving her a perpetual cynical appearance. But that conveyed a totally false impression about her outlook. Her nose was on the flat side with wide nostrils and her otherwise dentist-perfected white upper set of teeth held on to a marginal overbite in spite of the doctor's efforts to obliterate it. But it induced a pout in a shapely mouth that could suggest naivete or come-on to the eyes and mind of whoever beheld it. Most men beheld the latter. But Seema was not an indiscriminate flirt. Her large liquid dark brown eyes joyously looked out from beneath black eyebrows that tended towards heaviness and, consequently, required careful and tiresome plucking to keep them in pleasing shape. Her singular most striking feature was a rich head of long silky black hair that she swept away from a wide forehead and let fall luxuriantly around her square shoulders and just below her waist. Seema was of medium height that covered a bulk not dissimilar to Shahana's, although her waist was not disfigured by any unseemly fat. She did not look voluptuous, but men lusted for her. Her walk, not at all practised, brought out the primeval sexual instinct in them. Her entire body seemed to undulate as her widish hips rhythmically swayed like a classical Indian dancer in performance. She was a classical Indian dancer, or, rather, had been.

There are several teachers of classical Indian music and dancing in Britain and North America. Some of them had been quite well known in Bangladesh, India or Pakistan where they came from. Others were not so famed, but were trained and had performed to limited audiences at home. Then they had migrated, with most of the women artistes joining immigrant husbands, and had opened up schools, fair-sized and small, to earn money, keep in touch with their art and to disseminate it among the locals. Seema's artistically-inclined parents had sent their only daughter, when she was seven, to one of the better dancing schools that was run by an Indian couple. For almost ten years she learnt the intricacies of the complex Indian classical dancing without ever mastering them enough to become a high-class performer in South Asia. Her teachers attributed her shortcoming to heaviness of feet. But she participated in front of generally appreciative audiences in a number of public and private shows in the less demanding atmosphere of the expatriate community. She never lost the sinewy rhythm of dance in her normal movements. The expatriates adulated her when Shahana first met her and noticed the congregation of men around the bubbly personality. She also noted that the young girl was handling all that attention with easy grace and great charm. She played no favourites with any one, but did not offend anyone either. Shahana would not even have social interaction with any of Seema's admirers, all of Bangladeshi origin, but she wanted that girl to be her friend and confidante. She had heard about her artistic success from her parents and other relatives, but she found the person behind the reputation to be a wonderful human being.

The two did establish rapport, met and talked over the phone quite regularly and Seema learnt of her new friend's distaste for South Asian men and for the Bangladeshi expatriate society. But she never learnt about her loss of virginity. Shahana did not trust her enough to keep to herself the revelation of a striking event in her life. After all, she did mix a lot with the Bangladeshi community and even if she inadvertently let out this information, it would quickly become common knowledge. That would be disaster. Shahana also learnt that Seema preferred the company of South Asians, especially Bangladeshis, although she had a number of white and black male and female friends. She explained that she felt more comfortable in the South Asian culture. She loved the music and the sub-culture and the easygoing ways of the people, especially the Bengalis. She liked the way the Bengalis project a happy façade while inside they are suffering from worry and turmoil, how, when they are really happy, they are the very definition of the term happiness.

Then the two young women passed their A-levels and were getting ready to enter university life. And Shahana was considering telling Seema about her sex life. And learn hers in return. She had no idea why she wanted to do that except for some vague notion that the shared knowledge would somehow bring them closer. She felt the need for a close woman friend of her own ethnic background. Then that prospective close friend chose to get married. To a friend of her oldest brother. Seema had two big brothers, the oldest a dozen years older than her. Which is how she met her future husband. He was her brother's closest friend and she had known him since he had first come to their house. She was six then; he had just started studying engineering with her brother at the same university. Her brother married and moved out of the house; she grew up and got noticed by the friend as something other than a little kid to be ignored most of the time. She was flattered when he first started showing attention, then fell in love with him and, within a year of their new awareness of each other, married him. With full parental and brotherly consent. He was tall, handsome, quiet and introspective, was a qualified systems engineer, had his own successful computer business and a good-sized house, was polite and well-behaved and was very much in love with Seema. There was a grand wedding to which Shahana went with her family, but her plan for greater intimacy vanished. Shahana was stupefied when Seema told her the news but kept all the obvious questions bottled up inside her. The two kept in sporadic touch.

Seema moved to her husband's house only a kilometer or so from her father's. The dancing stopped and the singing began. The dancing stopped because she wanted it to. She gave birth to a cute daughter within a year of marriage and most of her time went towards caring for her. Dancing was out of the question. She put on hold indefinitely her higher education plans as she concentrated on being a full-time housewife and mother. A big part of her day was spent at her parents'. They enjoyed having their only daughter and granddaughter around.

Their married sons only had a bunch of boys. When her daughter was three, Seema took up singing. Her father arranged for her lessons at his house, five evenings a week. The *Ustad* was a Pakistani immigrant who specialized in light classical Urdu ghazals. He was good in his own right, but with Mehdi Hassan, Ghulam Ali and a host of high-class ghazal singers dominating the scene in his country, he could not make it there beyond minor recognition. He came over to England, not because he wanted to make a greater name for himself there, but for greater financial opportunity through business enterprises. He became a fairly successful businessman and turned to picking up his passion — music. A music school inevitably followed, the business enterprises were left in the hands of sons and nephews, and Seema's lessons started. She was taught the fundamentals of classical Indian music and she taught herself Bengali songs. She was not good, her teacher thought, but encouraged her because her father was his friend and a steady income flowed from that source. Her father now wanted her to be established in the expatriate community as a singer and, after a succession of failed public performances in Bengali songs, asked her to concentrate exclusively on ghazals. She had failed in the songs, which she enunciated in the Sylheti accent, of her own domestic language, and she failed in the rendition of the songs of another language. She would not have succeeded in the decent singing of songs of any language. She simply did not have the voice, and she was aware of that and told her father so, but she persevered to while away the time at the parental home.

Once a week her father arranged a musical evening at his house for ten to twenty people. Most of the guests were Bangladeshis, and they were served a good dinner and an assortment of songs. The *Ustad* was always present and was the chief attraction with his songs. Seema sang too. She was much more comfortable in the informal, intimate and familiar setting and did not care what anyone thought of her singing. In the relaxed atmosphere she actually performed better than usual. At one of these musical soirees, well into her fifth year of marriage, she met Riaz Hossain, a Bangladeshi who had migrated a long time ago. And started to have an affair with him. He was more than twice her age at forty-eight, married, with grown-up children. He was her father's friend and used to address him as "uncle" — until they started the affair. The form of address is common in Bangladeshi tradition, where elders are either "uncles," or "brothers" or "sisters," generally according to the age gap between the two groups. It was her first extra-marital affair; he had gone through a few during his twenty-four years of marriage. By training a physician, he had abandoned practice a long time ago to become a wealthy businessman. His wife knew about his periodic philandering through the grapevine and resigned herself to apathy. By nature a quiet, unassuming person, she devoted herself to bringing up their two daughters. They were grown up, the eldest a social welfare officer, the younger studying to become a doctor. She found solace in their achievements and looked forward to the days when she would become a good mother-in-law and a doting grandmother.

Seema and her lover would often meet at her place, during the day, when her husband would be tending to his business and her daughter would be pampered at her grandparents'. Seema would have her husband drop her over there on his way to work, giving the excuse that she required peace and quiet to complete a load of housework. Then she would await Riaz's arrival and, almost in no time, was making intense love on the bed she shared with her husband. She discovered that her passion for him was turning into a deep love and did not know how to handle the situation. She decided to confide in Shahana who, a year and a few months earlier, had introduced her to the eighteen plus a few months old Nabila.

Nabila Khan was a stunning beauty. A slender figure, smallish stature and large innocent-looking eyes gave her a fragile appearance that needed continuous protection and care. She was anything but fragile, although she was prone to occasional depression arising out of emotional vulnerability. Otherwise she was mentally a tough young woman who, at the age of eighteen, did not know quite what she wanted out of life, but carried out with determination anything that she finally decided on doing. She toyed with the idea of modeling for South Asian fashion shows and magazines. Nabila was under no illusion that, at five feet four, she had the height to be a Western catwalk model. But neither was she under any doubt that she was a beauty who could model for South Asian fashion shows and was photogenic enough to grace the pages of glossy magazines. She gave it a shot during the time she decided that she would wait a year before enrolling in a university. Then, when on the verge of making a breakthrough, she backed off. During this year of taking a break from formal education, she also briefly flirted with the idea of taking short courses to try becoming an actress. Again, just before paying enrollment fees to a good short duration acting school, she abandoned the idea of entering the entertainment world.

Nabila had a small narrow face with high cheekbones, a perfectly shaped straight nose, a firm chin and soft inviting lips. Her wide-set large black eyes with long upward-curving eyelashes beneath a pair of arched eyebrows that almost touched in the middle gave her a look of a Pakistani or a North Indian. She did have Pakistani ancestry on her father's side of the family. Her black hair, silky and with gentle wave in it, was finely combed back from a slightly sloping forehead down to her exquisitely narrow waist. She walked with long strides, always with a pensive look on her face, and her beautifully proportioned hips swayed to her pedestrian motions. Whenever out in public, she would always fling her handbag over her right shoulder. Her skin tone was light brown, but of a shade darker than Shahana's, and her jet black hair, black eyes and almost-joint eyebrows made her appear even a little more dark when she stood next to her brown-haired, light coloured-eyed friend.

Nabila lived with her parents in a modest two-bedroom apartment in Vauxhall. Not too long ago they resided in a sumptuous house and had two cars. Then her father was a high-ranking executive of a multinational company. One day the company crashed and he was out of a job. His shattered psyche took a long time to recover and had a sobering effect on his daughter, an only child. She was ten at that time and was introspective even then. Her parents' agony further made her withdraw into her shell, and their battle for years with relative poverty, which she shared in, also made her tough. Gradually, he started a small business in Vauxhall and rented the small apartment they now called home, but could not afford to maintain a car. He had sold off the two he had a long time ago to help keep the family out of abject distress.

Nabila's father had migrated to England out of a whim to live there. He belonged to a traditional upper-class family of Dhaka, was married to a lovely woman from a similar social background, was independently well-off, had an MBA from Dhaka University and was a highly-paid senior executive in a private business firm. He belonged to the rarefied social circle of the privileged class and participated in all the activities of that set. Then he decided to settle in England, just for the fun of it. He was offered the lucrative job he later crashed out of by a relative who was the personnel chief of the company. One evening, when Nabila was two, he boarded a British Airways flight with her and his wife and left Dhaka behind for good. In the thriving old days he came back for visits each year, and Nabila had annual re-acquaintance with a culture that she was never going to be an integral part of. With the coming down in monetary circumstances, the visits ceased altogether and Nabila had to rely on visiting relatives to brush shoulders with the latest trends in ancestral traditions. She discovered that they did not change much.

Nabila, like Shahana and Seema, did not have any objection to making an occasional short visit to Bangladesh. It was just another tourist destination with the added bonus of being adulated upon by relatives, close and far. She found that touching, if a little overwhelming, but the call of London soon made her restless to get away from all the disadvantages of Bangladesh. Nabila, until she could not afford to go there, had discovered a strange phenomenon in Dhaka. Her relatives there were, in many ways, more liberal than her parents in London were. Her parents were quite strict, regulating her social life and, when she turned nineteen, almost succeeding in marrying her off to an expatriate Bangladeshi specialist physician. She had not made any outright objection, but, after having met him for several weeks, decided that he was not the right man, told her parents so, and succeeded in persuading them to call off the marriage. Strange, she reflected, how they had gone for an arranged marriage for their daughter. They had married after a protracted love affair in Dhaka. Yet, in London, they had become very conservative, looking to religion and old traditions for solace and as a defense mechanism against Western culture in its home setting that they found difficult to accept. It was so much easier to adopt that culture as an instrument of appearing trendy in the poverty-ridden traditional society of Bangladesh. Nabila had heard similar stories from her friends — that their liberal parents from socially conservative Bangladesh had turned conservative in socially liberal Britain. But so did a number of her friends and acquaintances who were born and raised in Britain. Nabila was going to let social scientists determine the rationale behind that. She was going to deal with less profound issues.

Like having a good time behind her watchful parents' eyes. She was lucky to have a divorced aunt living on her own close by. This was a free spirit who understood her niece's dilemma of having to break some of the strictures set by parents whom she otherwise obeyed. The aunt was in her early thirties, having a riotous time in London, and providing protection for her niece. She simply informed her brother and sister-in-law that their daughter was visiting her when actually she was somewhere else. Like with a boyfriend. Nabila had no preference for men in terms of race and ethnicity. It was just a coincidence that she had been with blacks and Pakistanis more than any other ethnic types. She was careful in terms of sexual relations though. She was not a virgin, but she had been to bed with just two of her beaux. The last, about the time when she had first met Seema, had been with a black man, with whom she had fallen in deep love. She had broken with him when her parents had arranged for the prospective doctor groom and she had given in to their wish of getting to know him better. But she suffered like she had never done before and was depressed for a long time. She had always performed the required minimum of Islamic religious practice — she fasted during Ramadan and prayed most of the time — but during this trying time she prayed five times a day and kept occasional non-binding fasts. And she accepted a part-time teller's job at a bank. Anything to forget the pain that only her intimates were aware of. Her aunt suffered with her. Her parents, although disappointed that their marriage plans for her had fallen through, were pleased to see that their daughter had turned more to religion and had found a job instead of being idle. They were even happier that the money she earned was going to pay for her higher education.

Nabila resumed academic life as an Economics student at a university of average standing. She was nineteen and had come out of her pain. She reverted to her normal minimum religious obligations and met Seema's husband. She had gone with Shahana to one of the intimate musical soirees where Seema dreadfully rendered a couple of Bengali Nazrul songs, but more passably a couple of modern Bengali ones. Her husband kept eyeing the gorgeous nineteen-year-old in a night-blue shalwar-kameez. Then mustered up the courage to talk to her. His wife was happy that her normally reticent husband had shed his reserve with her new friend. That friend found an intelligent man who showed her pleasant attention. She was flattered to be accepted into the inner extended family. He wanted to be in touch with her. She thought nothing was wrong with that. He kept more in touch with her than did his wife. And then that frequent contact over the phone (hers was exclusively the mobile, his primarily the office with the mobile in special situations) became physical as they fell in love. He was fascinated by her youth, beauty and sophistication; she by his intelligence and quiet maturity. They could not meet as often as they would have liked, but meet they did, for the most part at the bachelor apartment of an Indian friend of his. Lucky for her that university life meant a lot of free hours; lucky for him that he owned his business and had employees to cover for his suddenly more frequent business trips.

They made love and fell deeper in love. She knew what her parents' reaction would be if they got wind of her affair. Nabila, for once, did not confide in her aunt who assumed that her niece looked so happy because she had found a nice young man.

"Why won't you tell me who he is?"

"Maybe later."

"He must be special. You look terrific."

"He is."

So special that she did not know what the future held for them. Sometimes she felt guilty about what she had done to her friend, but her heart made her forget her guilt. He was in a deep quandary. He doted on his daughter and felt sorry for his wife and her family members who were always very nice to him, but he had no idea how to bring about a resolution to the problem of his own creation. "My heart's creation," he silently admonished himself.

Then the grapevine got wind of the affair. How, no one could exactly pinpoint. Both Nabila and her lover had been extremely cautious about their clandestine meetings. He was certain that the Indian friend could be completely trusted to keep their secret. Or, could he? Maybe they had been seen together by some Bangladeshi who had quickly put two and two together. Maybe it had been someone from Nabila's university. However the news got out, it hit the grapevine. But even that formidable channel was not sure enough to be able to spread anything more definitive than that the married man had taken a fancy to a beautiful young woman. However vague, it was still juicy enough to titillate imaginations and, along the grapevine route, reached Seema's ears. At first, she dismissed it as another baseless rumour. Then she started close scrutiny of her husband, his attention to her, and his work habits. She found that he had become distant from her without ever being offensive in his manners and that he was taking frequent business trips from his office. Then intuition told her that the grapevine was right. She had to know the identity of the woman, and this was no easy task, but eventually she did. Again, there was no concrete evidence for her to confront her husband and she started to brood and lost a sizeable portion of her vivacity. When her lover came along she gave in, but Nabila's betrayal continued to haunt her. She decided to go to Shahana.

"You introduced her to me."

"So it's my fault! I didn't introduce her to your husband."

"But you knew the kind of person she is."

"She's a wonderful person. She's always nice to me."

"You don't have a husband she could steal."

"And your husband didn't go for her?"

They realized that they were going nowhere with their conversation, that they were only being driven apart from one another. They did not want that. And Seema had in the first place come to open her heart to her friend. Shahana had no idea that Nabila was having her affair. She did not tell her and she could not be bothered to ask her about her love life. Moreover, they only met occasionally. Now she also heard about Seema's affair.

"You people are in a real mess now, aren't you?" was all she could think of to say to her unhappy friend. She could only suggest that Seema should break up her own affair. But that would not help get her husband back and Nabila would continue having him.

Seema left and went back to her lover whom she could neither leave nor have for her own. He was not going to divorce his wife for a temporary fling. She knew that very well. Her husband was thinking of divorcing his wife to marry his lover. He was telling Nabila of this plan but she kept discouraging him and he could not understand why.

"Wait a little longer. You got to be sure you really want me."

She knew he did, as much as she wanted him, but she was thinking of her parents. And their expectations from her. And then she was thinking that their affair could not be kept bottled up forever. Sooner or later the grapevine would know and so would her parents. She could not talk to anyone about the quagmire she was in, not even to her aunt. And Shahana was out of the question.

Shahana was busy planning for her date with Alec, the scientist from her work place who had asked her out. He was in his late thirties, recently divorced and looking for some company. This was new territory for her. All her previous encounters were with men who were never married, at least none had admitted to any, and were mostly about her age. She was excited. She would let time decide what the future with Alec would be. If there was going to be a future. At the moment, she was just going to have a good time.

Notting Hill Nocturnal

There is this pub in Notting Hill Gate. So what? There are lots of pubs in Notting Hill Gate. And any pub is as good, or as bad, or as indifferent, as the other. Not quite. Each pub has its own little defining characteristics, but, all right, there is something to the point that every pub is as good.... Thus spake my friend Arvind Bhatia, he of the brushed-back pony-tailed hair, rakish looks, disarming philosophy of life, and of a heart of pure gold. He was setting me straight on my puny knowledge about the intricacies of pub character. He should know. He was working in one. And at that pub in Notting Hill Gate, to be precise.

I was staying at one of the reasonably priced hostels around the Notting Hill Gate tube station. So did an assortment of mostly young men and women from, it seemed, every white country in the world. South Africa and Zimbabwe are not white, but I ran into a few of their citizens and they did not represent the majority race. Wonderful people, those southern Africans. Occasionally I noticed a face that had my own brown colour, but I suspected they were British, either through birth or through immigration. That was my first impression, but, as Notting Hill Gate grew on me, I was proven only partially right.

Babel is in Notting Hill Gate tube station and its vicinity. A delightful cacophony of languages reaches one's ears as soon as one gets off the train and stays with one up the stairway and out on to the main street and in its surroundings. Americans make up a generous portion of the foreigners who temporarily inhabit that part of London. Like yours truly, an American immigrant in his early thirties, who was in the British capital for carrying out historical research. I found the reasonably priced habitation and settled in for a year. The relative scarcity of brown faces was equally matched by the paucity of black faces. Didn't any black or brown tourist know about the attractions of

Notting Hill Gate? There must be something in the area to draw so many white tourists. Or, was it that Notting Hill Gate had turned into a tradition that was followed by succeeding batches of tourists who would be certain to meet fellow citizens?

Certainly there is the Portobello Road market for Saturdays and every other day, and the annual Notting Hill Gate carnival. This carnival was held during my stay and I can well believe the organizers' claim that it is the biggest carnival outside of Brazil. There one sees many South American faces and even more black ones. They give vent to the rhythm of their exuberant spirit and the rest of the world rejoices with them. And a good number of the blacks do not come from far off either. As I discovered, while there were few blacks living around the vicinity of the Notting Hill Gate tube station, you could find them in good numbers only a little distance away, at Shepherd's Bush, for example. And around the Portobello Road market. Every Saturday a muted carnival takes place along Portobello Road. It is only muted in terms of lower decibel levels and the intensity and frenzy of body movements of the Notting Hill Gate carnival. Everything is so relative. Saturdays from the Notting Hill Gate tube station to the Portobello Road market is a continuous procession of people that become a massive entity that emits a powerful pulsating festive heartbeat and a single drone of many intermingling voices. For about ten hours, starting at around ten in the morning, every Saturday, Portobello Road market becomes one human being.

Portobello market is open on other days, but it is humdrum, routine, selling daily essential, mainly food, items at reasonable prices. But the Saturday revelers, including the temporary stall owners hawking seemingly every merchandise imaginable, are absent. I have been to these revelries, pushed along by an irresistible force of humanity from behind, more to soak in the atmosphere and to join in the merrymaking than to make any significant purchase. But I have made more trips on the quiet days to buy the essential goods necessary for my daily sustenance. And that is how I became aware of the Bangladeshis in Notting Hill Gate. The unmistakable sounds of dialect Bengali hit my ears as I was about to enter a meat shop run by Pakistani immigrants who spoke Punjabi among themselves, Urdu with other Pakistanis who did not understand Punjabi, and English with all others. The Punjabi, Urdu and English receded into the background as the familiar sounds of dialect Bengali rattled off in staccato bursts by three voices introduced me to the existence of men and women from my country of origin in a special London mecca heavily frequented by Western pilgrims. Curiosity led to the discovery that they, and other Bangladeshis, lived in close proximity to my hostel. And it took a chance encounter in a Pakistani butcher shop to learn of it. Pembridge Gardens ran parallel to the street that I lived in. Among its many buildings, almost all catering to housing foreigners, is the unpretentious Bangladesh Centre.

Once I had sniffed out the Centre I had to know it better. And I did — the exterior, the interior, the officials who ran it, the temporary guests who occupied it. The place is generally squalid, the communal kitchen the sufferer of the miseries inflicted on it by its array of users (and abusers), the bathrooms and toilets a mockery of sound hygiene, but it is a cheap shelter for Bangladeshis visiting London. Both the low price and the refuge are a big blessing to the sojourning Bangladeshis who tend to overlook a few days' inconvenience of the Centre's insipid services. And a small number forayed into Arvind Bhatia's other world — the pub in Notting Hill Gate halfway up Portobello Road going towards the market. As I did, two or three times a week.

My initiation into Arvind's other world came about as a result of a conversation with one of the sojourning Bangladeshis who had made a visit to that world. To hear and see him talk about his experience made it obvious that he had been impressed beyond his expectation and that it was his first acquaintance with a nude bar. He was returning to his country in a few days' time, but he was going back a very happy man. He would become the centre of rapt attention to inwardly or outwardly smirking audiences of friends and acquaintances (and a few selected relatives as well). His tale of the pub interested me less than the fact of its existence in close proximity. I had already been to the most sought-after strip joint in London, Stringfellow's, and had been suitably impressed by its attractions, but its very size and popularity made it, for me, less intimate than I would have liked. Besides, it was a fair distance from Notting Hill Gate and, consequently, not an irresistible temptation for a casual habitue of naughty bars. I had been to similar nightspots in New York and Boston to know that I would never become an addict. But the nearness of the pub and my natural inquisitive spirit inevitable led me to explore it.

The pub certainly tried its best to be discreet — no garish neon lights, no razzle-dazzle painted signs on its large outside glass windows, a pleasing and very chaste-sounding name — but it betrayed its existence by the small blackboard positioned outside its main entrance announcing in coloured chalks "Live Dancing." The exterior was painted a dull brown and heavy curtains across the windows hid the inside from probing outside eyes during the dancing hours. Early evening was well under way when I entered and my eyes had to adjust to the usual pub lighting inside — kind of murky, made hazier still by the crisscrossing patterns of thick smoke being emitted by a couple of dozen or so cigarette buffs. I registered the dance music blaring out in tolerable decibel level from all around as I zeroed in on the bar. An unoccupied stool was soon stoically suffering the pressure of my upper body as I surveyed my surroundings to the accompaniment of smoke from my own cigarette.

Wood paneling covered the walls of the large rectangular room halfway up where it gave way to off-white paint. The entire side opposite the bar was lined with cheap leather sofas that seated patrons preferring lax pleasure. Small low tables for supporting drinking glasses and ashtrays were intermittently positioned in front of them as were, at a respectable distance, three high round tables with four wooden chairs surrounding each one of them. If necessary, one of the chairs could be shoved to one side and the table brought closer to a sofa to accommodate large groups of people. The bar itself was the usual run-of-the-mill enclosure that one sees in any moderately good pub. It featured a reasonably large selection of drinks. Around and behind the bar was the toilet that, as I experienced later, stank from the discharge of hard-drinking patrons unable to hold the liquid within themselves. Across from its entrance door and clearly from the bar was a raised platform covered in plush red carpet with a narrow cylindrical steel pipe going down through its centre to the ground and pushing up through the ceiling and disappearing into it. This is where the girls did much of their dancing.

One was dancing as I walked in. I got to know her from subsequent visits. She was an Israeli, on the right side of twenty, and, boy, could she gyrate! Wow! Wow! Wow! She knew how to pump up the passion of even the most jaded of men. Hell, she had my attention all right. She finished her routine and was shortly replaced by another twenty-something, an attractive Venezuelan. But, hell, hell, hell! Her charms did not extend to her dancing. She was, oh, so listless, so mechanical, so soporific that I frantically looked for the bartenders and some stiff brew. Actually, almost as soon as I had first settled in, the barmaids drew my attention. At least, one of them did, with a pleasant "What will you have, sir?" I looked into the eyes of a thin blonde with a pretty face and sad pale-blue eyes. Two other girls, rather plain-looking, were busily taking care of the other customers. They were all sweaty from their grind, but never for a moment projected anything other than pleasant efficiency. At some point, when I was fortified with a few pints and been alternatively lifted to ecstasy by the Israeli and plunged into despair by the Venezuelan, a gravelly voice with more than a trace of a South Asian accent was addressing me: "You all right?" I was peering into the face of Arvind Bhatia.

Arvind Bhatia was arresting. He was in his early thirties, of medium height, powerful build and a hawkish face. Every once in a while he would take off the rubber band that held in place the pony tail — to air out his hair, Arvind would explain — and a shock of released shoulder-length wavy dark brown hair prancing behind his neck with every movement of his head transformed his looks into one of a wild spirit. A pair of wide-set, greenish-brown eyes always seemed to be twinkling with amusement. But to take them at their face value could be a mistake. Arvind had a heart of gold, but he was deadly serious at his work. He had to be. He was the supervisor of a nude bar. That pub on Portobello Road that the owner tried his best to make unobtrusive, but inevitably failed to stem the flow of a torrent of revelers almost every evening. The owner was a Greek-Cypriot immigrant who spent most of his time looking after his taxicab business and who generally arrived when the pub was about to close down for the day at eleven at night. Then he would talk business with his manager and Arvind and depart with the day's earnings. He left it to the manager to pay the daily and weekly wages. But he did not trust the manager. He trusted no one. So he hired Arvind to keep an eye out on the cash till, the bartenders and the manager. And Arvind was in no doubt that he had asked the manager to keep an eye out on the cash till, the bartenders and the supervisor.

"Slimy bastard," was the best that my friend could bring himself to talk about his "guv'nor" in terms of endearment. And not just because of his distrustful nature. He also was not generous with his wages, especially since the employees had to put in an inordinate amount of work almost each evening. No wonder the barmaids (he instructed his manager to only hire women) tried (and sometimes, no doubt, succeeded) to lighten the cashbox for their "guv'nor." "To tell you the truth," Arvind let me in on his expansive heart, "I might be tempted to do the same if I were them." But he was not them; he was their supervisor, hired to keep an eye on them to prevent what sometimes he privately thought they did no wrong in doing. He was deadly serious in his job. But that slimy bastard made it trying. He simply could not keep his misshapen podgy hands off the dancing girls he fancied. The girls expected slavering men in their line of work and were past masters at keeping them at bay, as most of them did the "guv'nor." A lot of them even did not know that he was that, but it did not matter. They knew the manager and the supervisor, one of whom paid them at the end of their nightly performance. Occasionally the owner succeeded, although his manager warned him that he could bring trouble on himself and the establishment. But he did not care. He had to have fun in his life. All work and no play.... He scored more consistently with the barmaids whose turnover frequently was also high.

"So why don't you quit?"

"I like the work. Great fun. Get to meet some characters. And the girls are all right." He liked the dancers — for the most part — there were a few bitches who showed up now and then and whose agency manager was then asked not to send them again — but primarily for their pleasant disposition, their dancing, and their consummate skill in keeping at bay a roomful of concupiscent men while lightening their pockets with sweet smiles pregnant with double entendre. Each dancer would have her own strip routine and would titillate the patrons several times during the evening. Two would appear every evening and take turns dancing to the beat of their selected musical pieces until closing time heralded the end of their hard work and the patrons' revelry. Money, in the meantime, had flown out of the customers' pockets to the bar and the dancers.

The patrons, with a caveat, were always male, of various ages, including, every so often, evergreen septuagenarians wanting to fade into eternal winter with the memory of erotic spring, and of varied professions, all bonded in a primordial male instinct. But the clientele was not all men. The pub was divided into two sections, of which one had the dancers with the male patrons. The other, with its own entrance, had its own bar and did not offer its customers any view of the action on the adjoining side. The customers did not want any, either. And the majority here was also men. They were there to have a quiet drink, or to shoot pool — their interest was solitude. A few women, mostly with male partners, turned up in this section. So did gays.

But the frenzied and boisterous action was on the other side of the spacious wooden divide. At the end of each dance, the dancer, who had bared all only a few minutes earlier and now with some sort of covering, went around to each patron with a collection jar. Almost everyone deposited a least a pound coin in it. A few demurred, others offered a drink instead, or on top, of the money, still others beat a hasty retreat as soon as a number ended to avoid paying anything. However, most patrons were generous, especially to the dancer who caught their fancy. Thus, almost invariably, there were unequal earnings among the dancers. Arvind confided that the pub paid each the incredibly modest sum of ten pounds, and offered no drink on the house. But they could keep all their tips and they made a good amount that way. They seemed to come from all over the globe, except South Asia. I never saw one from that part of the world and Arvind assured me that he had not either.

Most of the dancers were in their early twenties, generally nice looking and friendly. Some were university students trying to earn enough to pay for their higher education. Others were in it for the pure thrill of it all. Some appeared to be embarrassed at having to be exhibitionists; most rejoiced at being able to be so.

Arvind was a student of human character as much as he was a character himself. People liked him. Steady patrons sought his company, even if it was only for a brief moment. The bartenders found a warm, tough, but fair, boss whom they liked having around. The manager became a good friend and once, to the delight of many customers and consternation of a few, an American dancer caught hold of his hand and danced with him. No, Arvind would not quit this job for a while yet. Or, maybe he would. I did not know him well enough to determine with certainty his intentions. Our interactions remained restricted to the bar. He was obviously a loner whose gregariousness was situational. Maybe I was mistaken in this judgement. The thing was that I wanted to get to know this intriguing person better. For that to happen I had to become a close friend. The recluse must have close friends, I thought. He had. Not many, but they existed. And one evening I met them. And learnt their stories some time later from him.

They were a motley group of South Asians. Three immigrants and a tourist. The odd one was a frequent visitor to qualify as a quasi-immigrant. He had spent his youth in London on the way to qualifying as a Chartered Accountant. He then went back to Bangladesh, his home country, to take over his father's substantial business interests and reduce — modestly — their value. He never thought of applying for British immigration, but had bought a house in Chiswick. He married his childhood sweetheart, had two sons whom he left mostly to his wife to supervise and took to heavy bouts of drinking to ease the pain of gradual realization that his wife was a diehard materialist who shared none of his passion for the high arts. He had a brief fling, but continued to co-exist with his wife. Well, he conceded to himself, she was a shrewd and hardworking businesswoman who brought in the money. He lived well off it. He barely tolerated her. And made annual trips to London. There he met up with old friends like two of the immigrants he was with at the Notting Hill bar.

Both these immigrants were also Chartered Accountants, one of Bangladeshi, and the other of Pakistani, origin. All three had studied together, but the two Bangladeshis had known each other from the time when they were teenagers in the waning days of East Pakistan. The expatriate Bangladeshi had married a white English woman and had prospered with three children and a generous yearly income. The Pakistani, after years of philandering, had finally decided to settle down in his forties by marrying a lovely British Hindu woman of Indian origin, almost twenty years his junior, and becoming a father at the age of forty seven. Arvind knew these two and got to know the visitor for the first time that evening. I was an acquaintance of the Bangladeshi from my infrequent visits to my ancestral homeland and was introduced for the first time to his friends that same evening. And all of us met, for the very first time, the third immigrant, a Pakistani in his early fifties, Arvind's good friend, who came in after all of us had settled in and were halfway through our first drinks. He was a character, a smooth talker and obviously a bit of a con artist, who enlivened the rest of the evening well into the night, but I met another interesting person who had left before any of this group had first strolled in at around nine. He was another of Arvind's dizzyingly numerous acquaintances and he had come in seven and had departed an hour or so later.

"What did you think of him?" Arvind inquired once he had made his exit.

Something in his voice put me on guard.

"Haven't yet. Why?"

"Man, the more you see of people, the more surprised you get." Which was not exactly a revelation, but my friend was voicing the truism from his heart. Arvind, the eternal optimist, leaned towards the good in human beings, but he gave me the distinct impression that he did not like the subject of our discussion.

The subject, a man in his mid-forties, was a Bangladeshi Muslim immigrant who lived around Notting Hill Gate. He never tired of proclaiming to his community (and to anybody listening) that he could drink almost anybody under the table. Wow! The Bangladeshi community thought him cool. At least most did. Those who did not did so either because they strongly disapproved of a forbidden act in Islam, or because they suspected him to be a con artist out to score points to further his own ulterior designs. And being seen to be a debonair man who could hold his drink with the best of them was one of his strategies.

He could certainly talk though. He had me convinced that he was a leader in his community and had all these wide connections in Bangladesh. He had left a high-paying executive job in Dhaka because the city was getting too small for his multitudinous talents. Now he was an established businessman who liked to frequent bars. He was smartly dressed and had this restless, affected air about him, but that did not bother me. What struck me as odd was that this denizen of the pub did not order a single hard drink during the time we were at our table.

"I have to be at a party later on. There's going to be plenty of drinking there, you know." I did not know, but maybe he was fortifying himself with three glasses of orange juice to conquer the hard stuff later.

"The bugger doesn't drink," Arvind educated me. "Know why he comes?"

"Educate me."

"To look at the dancers."

"So does everyone else."

"But they tip them well. And they buy a lot of drinks. Real ones. The sonofabitch gets a glass, maybe two, of juice and nurses that for a whole hour. And all the time he is sneaking glances at the girls. Doesn't even look at them straight."

It was an unusual evening because he had three glasses in my company. I was beginning to happily muse at the impression I must have created to have induced such an extraordinary reaction when Arvind's words abruptly cut it short.

"He's married with a kid. Married his cousin. She's British by birth." People adopt a variety of strategies to gain residence in their country of choice. Nothing unusual in the last Arvind offering. A number of South Asians, not to say men and women of other nationalities, take recourse to that ploy. It was an unusual night, though. The dancers that evening were both English, both red-haired, one a fragile-looking beauty, the other buxom, more robust, but with a carnal attractiveness about her. The delicate dancer had two tiny golden ringlets perforating the upturned rosy nipples of her small shapely breasts, a bigger one of the same metal ornamenting her belly button and a small diamond stud penetrating her clitoris. That looked ghastly, but she reassured me that she had had it on for seven years, since the time she was fifteen, and it kept her in permanent rapture. Bet it did! Her sensuous dancing, coupled with an angelic face, earned her a lavish sum in tips.

She was in the middle of a number when the motley crew of three Chartered Accountants walked in, with sheepish grins and mincing steps. They looked very uncertain, wore worried looks, until Arvind greeted them and sat them at my table. Even then, unease never completely left them. Every so often they would sweep the entire pub interior with nervous eyes to ensure that no known face was around to later spread unwelcome gossip. Fortunately for them, that evening, they met no one they knew. That was their first visit to that pub, but I strongly suspect, it was going to be their last. They were sipping their drinks with intense concentration, darting quick glances at the dancers, and contributing in short spurts to the conversation when in walked, with impressive panache, the Pakistani in his early fifties. He was tall, balding, pockmarked, but remarkably well preserved for his years. He said he owned a talent agency for aspiring models, but I did not recognize its name. But, then, my knowledge about modeling agencies in general is severely limited. He started off with ribald jokes and quickly moved to the subject of women. He liked them between the ages of twenty and twenty-five and he preferred whites. The agency kept him happy.

Arvind excused himself to supervise for a stint and we ordered a fresh round of drinks. Then a white butt, ample and jiggling, loomed into our faces. Four pairs of eyes, popping out of four open-mouthed faces, were focussed on the owner of that derriere, now swiveling to reveal two voluptuous breasts, swaying majestically, from the gyrating body of the other redhead. You could touch those breasts with a short movement of a hand, but you were not allowed to. Which is when I spied Arvind among the crowd, looking in our direction, with a diabolical grin loudly proclaiming the cause of the visitation of "Busty Red" to our table. She said she went by the name of "Red" and was soon rubbing her behind across the talent agency owner's face. I marveled at his aplomb then and, even more, a bit later, when the gyrating figure plonked down on his knees and never lost a beat in its undulations. I looked on with interest, but the others were a compelling study in absolute discomfiture. God must have heard Himself being called under breath enough to have taken a pity on the three as the dancer parted company without having taken a move in their direction. She had other patrons watching and she had to fill her tipping mug.

Closing time arrived as the wall clock was hovering around the 11 p.m. mark. The dancers had closed shop and were waiting for their transports, and the patrons had thinned down to a smattering of hopeless lushes and diehard hangers-on. Then, they too were gone, mostly hustled out by the manager, a tall black man, and Arvind. The lights were dimmed or turned off altogether. Arvind invited us to stay for a relaxed last round of drinks before it was time to push off. After all the excitement, we were subdued and were just content to slowly sip our drinks over our own private thoughts. Which is when the sounds of commotion filtered through to our alcohol-befogged brain. They were coming from the direction of the bar where the manager and one of the bartenders, a twenty-something black woman, were having a heated argument. Gradually it dawned on us that he was accusing her of stealing from the cash counter. As the accusations got louder and more threatening, the protestations of innocence matched them in volume and then started to increase. The two then came out of the bar area and he backed her into a side wall, only a few yards from where we were sitting, now no longer in our own private reveries. Arvind made no effort to move; just watched. The situation looked ugly.

We were all waiting for the next escalation when it happened. The manager's long right hand had taken a vise-like grip on the woman's throat and was tightening on it, while his large eyes kept bulging till they seemed on the verge of popping out of their sockets altogether. She was clawing the air, emitting horrible croaking sounds, and her large eyes were also bulging, but they evinced the fright of death. Two of the Chartered Accountants were muttering to one another:

"Let's get out of here."

The fifty-something softly told the supervisor: "Do something. He's killing her!"

Arvind rushed towards the assailant and tried to separate his hand from her throat, all the while shouting for him to let go. He eventually did, and she went into a paroxysm of terrible coughs and stifled sobs. The pub went into total silence for a few long moments. I looked around. The assailant seemed to have had all the air sucked out of him and was flopping listlessly on the nearest sofa with Arvind having thrown an arm around him, calming him down. But he had calmed down once his hand of death had released its victim. The angry voice was now in bewildered silence. The Chartered Accountants had sagged back against their chairs, but the connoisseur of early twenties women was half standing, a tight noncommittal smile on his pockmarked face. The otherwise friendly visage had undergone a total transformation and it was sometime before it went back to its normal self. The other two female bartenders, who had watched the whole episode in silent apprehension, had rushed to their co-worker and were comforting her. Then the spontaneous silence was shattered:

"I'm calling the police." And the assaulted was staggering towards the pub pay phone. Arvind let go of his comforting arm around the manager and rushed towards her and placed the arm around her shoulders. In an instant he had foreseen the ramification of police intervention and tried to talk her out of her intent. For a long time, strongly urged on by the other bartenders, she would not budge from her position. Then she relented. Maybe she was just exhausted. Or maybe she was just happy to be out of her ordeal and get back to her young son at home. I learnt later that she was an unwed mother. He came and apologized. She just stared at him for a while and then turned to get her jacket and handbag from the storage space. It was time for her to go.

It was time for me to go too. Which I did. With the three Chartered Accountants and the agency owner. He suggested that we all go to a popular South Asian kebab house in the East End. It stayed open twenty-four hours a day and never failed to dish out the most delicious North Indian fare. Arvind could only bid us good night. He had a long few hours ahead of him. The manager was now leaning against the bar, a study of a mix of relief and anxiety. It was half an hour past midnight when we stepped out of the side entrance. We had to walk a bit to reach our parked cars. There were a few vehicles running on the street. The sidewalk was carrying the occasional pedestrian to whatever destination he/she was going to. Everything was so peaceful around us. And, although high summer was in progress, the chill of the surrounding air penetrated through the warmth of alcohol inside us.

Delusionals

Farukh Akbar walked into his sight while Max was in the process of taking an appreciative view of a stunning model-wannabe who was about to perch herself in front of him. He was not amused at being thus distracted. He was even less delighted when the interloper's anabasis carried him right next to the wannabe's chair and his breezy voice announced:

"My name is Farukh Akbar and I've an appointment."

This was too much for Max and he firmly, but courteously, pointed to a vacant chair a couple of metres behind and away from his table and instructed:

"If you would like to take a seat over there. I'll call you once I have attended to this young lady."

And, to himself, although he wished he could say it out loud: "Cheeky bastard! I don't want to see you."

Max — Maxwell d'Monte — could not figure out the reason for his instant dislike of Farukh, but he could not deny the fact of his feeling.

"The little motherfucker thinks he's cool. Thinks he's going to be a model! Isn't he in for a surprise!"

But so was the stunning model-wannabe. Because she had come to a rip-off agency in search of glamour and fortune and, possibly, fame. London houses a large number of modeling agencies that deal with the serious business of recruiting models and recommending them to their clients in the world of high fashion, cosmetics, clothing and similar ventures. Some of these agencies are high profile, others more low key, but all function in an intensely competitive environment. Weeds, however, have an unpleasant habit of taking root in the most manicured gardens. And in the modeling agency business, a few rogue companies crop up with the intention of making a quick buck at the expense of the stillborn hopes of others. Indeed, every minute is a sucker born.

Max was the manager of one of such shady agencies that went by the name of "Dream Face." The owner was a Pakistani immigrant, Mohsin Altaf, who had given up on a thriving "Indian" restaurant business to, as he rationalized, move up the social hierarchy by becoming the proprietor of a modeling agency. Now that would be exciting and carry with it his cherished perquisite: good-looking young women. By the time he opened his new business he was forty and had been divorced for two years from his white English wife of seven years, the mother of his two children. He had married her within the first year of arriving in Britain in 1978. He had fallen in deep love with her and the marriage provided him the added bonus of swiftly gaining his immigration papers. After the first few years of reasonably satisfying conjugal life, during which Mohsin had built up the thriving restaurant business and had fathered in quick succession the two children, things steadily started going downhill and culminated in his finding out that his wife was having an affair with their solicitor. A surprisingly amicable divorce followed, and Mohsin considered himself an unfettered bird, free to give wings to whatever desire goaded him. And his foremost fancy was to open a modeling agency and take his pick of the aspiring young women. Rumour had it that he had left behind a wife in his birthplace of Multan, and that they had a daughter who was in the care of his married sister's family in Rawalpindi. She was a cousin and their parents had arranged their marriage. Rumour also had it that he had sent her divorce papers from London, that she had since re-married and that he sent a fixed amount of money each month to his sister for his daughter's education and other expenses. And rumour had it that he talked as little as possible, to as few people as possible, about the girl, and that she intensely disliked her father. Those rumours, as Max had found out, were absolutely true. The manager had, within the relatively short period of a year that he was working at Dream Face, earned the trust and friendship of the owner. One evening, in an expansive mood and with a few glasses of red wine tucked inside him at a bar, Mohsin had told his manager the story of that part of his life.

Mohsin had started his new enterprise full of good intentions of making a splash in the cutthroat, but honest, modeling business. He had taken a medium-sized office space in trendy Covent Garden, had it equipped with the appropriate accessories, and had hired a very pretty young white secretary to provide it glamour and help. He had sold the two restaurants he owned to set up his new business and still had enough in the bank not to have to worry about making an immediate success in his new venture. But he did not even try to make it a success. He fell for his secretary who moved in with him and then, after a little over a year, left him and his business for a garage mechanic. By that time the budding business was in shambles and the owner was looking for a way to make a quick buck while retaining his enterprise of glamour and temptation. Thus was born in his head the idea of the rip-off agency. He had known about similar existing establishments and decided to emulate them.

But he had first to get out of Covent Garden. The establishment costs in that posh area were getting out of his reach and, in any case, he was apprehensive about running a shady operation in a high-profile locality. He found a cheap office space in a modest building in low-profile Fulham Broadway and began his transformed operations. For just over a decade now he had been a con artist of great charm and moderate financial success. The last year of those ten he had Max as a trusted associate and close confidante. Max did not know, until a few months into his work, that the organization he worked for was disreputable. Actually, he was sucked into it as a spared victim of the operation.

Max d'Monte had arrived in London three years ago from India on a short-term visitor's visa and had long overstayed his legitimate welcome. He was determined not to go back and was assiduously working towards getting immigration. He had left India with that intention in mind. He was twenty-eight when he had arrived in his chosen land of aspirations and the good life, but was under no illusion that his hopes would be realized any time soon or without considerable periods of anxiety and hard toil. Because he was a man of self-possession, he could reduce anxious moments to the status of minor irritations. And because he was not one to shy away from hard work, the prospect of prolonged drudgery did not daunt him. But equanimity and hard labour would not automatically bring him his cherished manna; he required good fortune and a lot of help. He thought he had found both at Dream Face.

Max was from Chennai (it was called Madras when he was born there), the descendant of a Frenchman and his Indian consort. The man had eventually gone back to his own country, leaving behind the woman to take care of and bring up two young children. In the tradition of South Asian women, particularly those of the early nineteenth century, she silently accepted her fate, quietly suffered through the inevitable social ostracism and concentrated on providing an education to her son and daughter. She was fortunate in getting free schooling for them from a local Irish-run missionary school. And she gained the satisfaction of seeing her almost inhuman labour at odd jobs being rewarded with her daughter reaching eighth standard and then getting married to an Anglo-Indian clerk, and her son matriculating and finding a job as a clerk in a British merchant shipping company. The d'Montes, purposeful and industrious, improved upon their lot with each succeeding generation and Max's father attained the position of senior engineer at the state electric supply authority. The son received a Bachelor's degree in Accounting and accepted a management position with a decent salary at a large private business concern. True to the d'Monte tradition, he had worked assiduously and was on his way to senior executive rank in the not too distant future. And then he threw away the assured financial security and status in the status-obsessed society of his country to plunge into the uncertainty of at all making it in the foreign land of his expectations. And only that factor — a singular determination to settle in Britain — made him pack up and leave.

He could not ask for better parents, had complete job satisfaction, a number of good friends and, at the time of his departure, was without a broken heart. He had, in fact, done more breaking than being on the receiving end of the jilting shaft. By temperament a rake, he was more intent on racking up the numbers of women he had seduced, but, once or twice, as if to re-invigorate his philandering wont through feeling a sense of aggrievement, he persuaded himself that women had unfairly spurned his eternal love. No, there was a whole lot for him to leave behind and, unless it was an atavistic reappearance of the wanderlust genes of his adventurous French progenitor, little reason to go off to the land that had for some time ceased being the mighty *raj*. Max's libidinous propensity certainly was a compelling factor, though. He was itching to have a go at white women "to broaden his experience," as he confided to close confidantes.

Well, he found London not as easy a hunting ground as he had imagined, but he did not remain a celibate there, either. Max was good looking, of medium height, big-boned and with a complexion that gave a clear indication of his European ancestry. His facial features were a happy compromise between the East and the West, square-jawed, thin-lipped, with large liquid dark brown eyes conveying impishness and sensitivity. They were set wide apart beneath thick black eyebrows and looked out from either side of a long straight nose with a fleshy tip. A firm square chin proclaimed a determined character just as a head of swept-back luxuriant black hair, stylishly maintained, hinted at a debonair spirit. His legs were rather skinny, but a narrow hip and a muscled waistline did much to disguise their incongruity in comparison with a well-structured upper body.

Behind the blithe appearance, however, was a man who would not spare himself from the details of any work he was undertaking. Max, as noted, was twenty-eight when he had arrived in London; he was thirty-one when Farukh Akbar had disagreeably walked into his view. In between he had worked at several jobs to survive and hunt for the legal work permit or immigration. These involved helping in the kitchen and waiting tables at several "Indian" restaurants, bartending at a pub run by an Anglo-Indian, and crunching numbers on the computer of an accounting firm owned by an Indian immigrant. Fortune favoured him when, soon after arriving in London, Max went to an Anglo-Indian party with the emigrated friend from back home with whom he was temporarily lodging. He met Kenny Rebeiro at the party, a man in his early forties, originally from Goa, but who had migrated with his parents over a quarter of a century ago. Kenny was a film producer who, after producing a number of documentaries from which he had gained satisfactory financial returns, was on the lookout for financiers to invest in a fairly large-budget full-length feature film in English. He would have nothing to do with Bollywood-type products, which he thought to be in poor taste and of mediocre overall quality. Thus far, over a period of two years of strenuous effort, he had only been able to raise about half of the projected outlay. And he was getting just a bit despondent.

Kenny did not lack the money to be able to live a comfortable life with a wife and two teenage kids. A retail clothing business saw to that, but he wanted to emulate the fame of Ismail Merchant. Maybe win an Oscar, or a BAFTA award. He was a dreamer, but was getting a bit restless for his vision to turn to reality. He took a liking to Max and learnt of that man's dreams.

"It won't be easy, but let's see what we can do about it."

Kenny could only do so much. His retail business did not need an extra hand, but he had contacts in the South Asian community. They were unwilling to take the risk of investing in his project for the fear of its failure, but many of them would welcome the opportunity to exploit cheap labour. Because that is what Max was in his status of limbo — a commodity to be hired and fired at will, treated like a bonded servant and paid in cash at a ridiculous rate that the payee knew was a swindle, but who had no choice but to swallow the pittance without protest. If he did not like it, well then, he was perfectly at liberty to leave.

"Take it or leave it. Be happy that you even have a job. I'm risking a lot by employing an illegal worker." Which was technically true. But technicality is not automatically implemented. The illegal worker can easily complain to the authorities about the unlawful practice of the slave driver. Which is easier said than done. Because the aggrieved party is not about to jeopardize his/her own agenda of eventually acquiring British immigration. And the employer knows this. The authorities are aware of the shady goings-on, but their awareness does not always translate into action. And so goes on the practice of employers being able to avoid paying a portion of their taxes by handing out measly sums of hard cash to employees who do not exist in Britain's registered workforce. As does their custom of maintaining a high rate of turnover of the easy-come-easy-go workers.

Max fit in nicely with the concept of the nomadic workingman. He was a workhorse who did not complain, was flexible both in terms of work hours and the nature of work, and silently accepted the taskmaster's giving him the sack. Mostly he drifted from restaurant to restaurant because these places always seemed to have temporary employment available and they also offered the chance to make some extra money in the form of tips. Although the restaurants advertised themselves as "Indian" serving "authentic north Indian" or all-encompassing Indian food, they were almost all owned by Bangladeshi expatriates or by entrepreneurs who were British by birth, but had Bangladeshi ancestry. The use of the more familiar term "Indian" was a pragmatic business ploy to attract clientele. It worked, unless the restaurant had acquired a poor reputation for serving execrable food, offering insufferable service and was located in an unfashionable area. Britain is not the tipping hotspot that the United States is, but is not a lifeless desert either, and Max saved the little bit of extra money that he earned. He was happier bartending because the atmosphere was more easygoing, even if the work was more hectic, and the clientele more interesting than at the restaurants, and he had a chance of going out with one or two of the female bartenders and satiate his priapic hunger. But the Anglo-Indian pub owner could not risk hiring him for more than a few days at a time and, so, Max found himself working at his favourite job only for short stints. The number crunching he found boring, both because he was far too qualified to be doing that and because the owner, originally from Mumbai, was a prosaic, miserly and choleric man who had turned his office into a funereal automaton. But the work allowed him to tide over his perpetual anxiety over income and he was grateful for that. Max could have asked for, and have received, some succour from his father, but he was too proud and independent to resort to that. Thus he continued to exist and hope.

Max had found a reasonably cheap one-bedroom apartment in Whitechapel. A long-time Bangladeshi expatriate owned it and provided the minimum services necessary to keep it just above slum-level. But the location in East London, with a strong Bangladeshi expatriate presence, had its advantages, being in proximity to most of the restaurants that he worked in and being within walking distance to shops selling moderately priced items for everyday use. And, delightfully, he could buy any of the spices that he craved for in the dishes that he cooked. He made a few Bangladeshi friends in the area and serendipity led to finding "Dream Face Modeling Agency." Max saw the advertisement in English in the open inside page of the local weekly newspaper in Bengali. He was visiting one of his new friends who subscribed to that paper to keep up with news about the Bangladeshi community in Britain and of happenings back in Bangladesh. Bangladeshis are an acutely sentimental people and the expatriates get easily nostalgic about the land they have left behind and to which most have no intention of permanently returning.

The advertisement was looking for new Asian faces to take on as prospective models. Max thought, with justification, that he was good looking and stood a chance of earning good money, and possibly fame, as a South Asian model. Thus he found himself face-to-face with, first, Natalie, the dyed-blonde pretty secretary with large breasts and an extra inch of waistline, and then with Mohsin Altaf himself. He was a smooth talker, that one, and Max was taken in by him. He found out later that he had equally impressed the owner. Max had made the appointment over the phone and went in smart casuals. He had taken extra care to groom his striking hair. He thought he looked good, and so did Mohsin.

"I'll make a portfolio for you for free. Come back next Friday with three sets of clothes."

Max was ecstatic and was even more so when he had gone through an hour's session of outdoor photo shoot, all made up and in different attires, in various poses suggested by the photographer who was none other than Mohsin Altaf himself.

Max did not know much about the art and science of photography and so had no idea about the professional expertise of his cameraman. When he went back a week later to have a look at his portfolio, though, he liked what he saw. But he was easily impressionable about things pertaining to himself. And the pictures, while definitely falling well short of the highest class, were still flattering enough to please Max. He was even more elated when Mohsin casually slipped in:

"Why don't you come to work for me? You can do it only once a week, and if you like it here, you can work more days," he hastened to add.

Max's head was in a whirl and the attractive model-wannabes sitting around for an interview almost made him lose his noggin altogether. Almost. He composed himself as best as he could:

"Let me do once a week. You know I'm working at the pub."

"I'll pay you more, but you decide what you want to do."

Max knew what he was going to do. He was already forgetting the female bartenders. Max had just completed a Faustian bargain behind the angelic façade of a job offer. He reported for work the following week on a day that the owner allowed him to select. And asked Mohsin the nagging question in his mind:

"When will I start modeling?"

"Soon. I've sent out your pictures to clients."

He would continue asking the question each week and the answer, after a point, changed in its contents:

"I don't know why they're not getting back to me," with an appropriate look of a mix of concern and commiseration, or, "Business is slack and they'll use the old models for now, but don't worry, you'll have your chance."

Several months would pass before he knew for certain that there were no clients, that his hopes for glamour and lucre would remain a mirage at Mohsin Altaf's hands. By that time he had quit being a bartender, restaurant worker and number cruncher and was working four days a week, for a steady pittance, as the manager of a small company that specialized in chicanery. He stayed on for the assured income, the variety of women he came in daily contact with, and in the hope that one day his employer would sponsor him for a permanent work permit. And he was grateful that Mohsin never asked him for his working papers. Maybe he had taken it for granted that Max had them, or, maybe, he did not care since he did not exist on his company records. Each week Max got paid in cash from a company income that was partly made up in almost non-traceable petty cash. But Max had not volunteered either in giving away his status in Britain to Mohsin. Which made it harder for him, as time went on, to broach the subject of sponsorship to his employer. But he was going to do it some day soon. Right then he was not going to rock the boat that was not rocking for him, and concentrate on his work of measuring, occasionally photographing, interviewing and chatting up the female model-wannabes who came his way. The male-wannabes, too, but he left their measuring and the chatting up to Natalie.

    The women seemed to come from every country in the world and ranged from short to very tall, over six feet, from plump to anorexic thin, and from plain looking who thought highly of their own looks to those who were truly beautiful. A very few had the attributes of becoming high fashion models, but many would not even get a casual consideration at the big talent agencies. But Dream Face granted an interview to anyone who was interested because they brought in the petty hard cash so vital to Max's physical, as well as mental, survival. Each day some fifteen mostly nervous young men and women came in and each paid ten pounds in cash only to have a set of four test shots taken to assess their photogenic qualities. They could have their pictures back, but most remained unclaimed to be trashed after a period of ninety days. The important thing was that, on an average, a cool one hundred fifty pounds in cash was collected each day when, as Max found out later, a small fraction of which would actually be spent towards washing and developing the pictures and paying the studio contracted to do the job at a bulk rate. The amazing thing was that hardly ever did anyone question the reason behind the prospective talent's paying for a service whose cost should logically be borne by the agency.

"Bloody suckers!" Max thought to himself. "They're so naïve and so eager to be models. Come to think of it, I'd have forked out the money if I had been asked!" But he had not been, and had received a free portfolio and a job offer in the bargain.

But some questioned having to pay for the portfolio. Now that is where the big scam took place. Mohsin would tape-measure a female interviewee's chest, waist and hip, lingering on just a bit longer on the bodies of those he fancied, and, following the test shots, he would have a talk with them that could last anywhere from five to twenty minutes. Mohsin used to conduct these interviews, but, as he began to rely more and more on his manager, he delegated that function to Max. These talks served the interviewer a dual purpose. He could chat up someone he took a fancy to and he could lure as many as possible to have a portfolio done and pay for the opportunity in the bargain. If the two men zeroed in on the women for personal preference, they made no discrimination between the sexes in selling their portfolio rigmarole. Because that is exactly what they would be offering: pledges that they could not possibly keep. They would be promised work for real houses of fashion that had not even heard of Dream Face and for advertising firms that Mohsin would not dare to introduce himself or his company to (oh, he was, of course, going to deduct a percentage of the model's earnings — it was the done thing, you know). The only thing was that the models required a portfolio from which Dream Face could periodically send pictures to its numerous clients. It would cost them 150 pounds, but they had to buy the portfolio book themselves. Of course, the company would be glad to help them select one.

Some would, with beatific smiles, then triumphantly produce a portfolio that they had already made for themselves. And Max's riposte would be a quick dismissive smile followed by a contemptuous comment on the quality, or lack thereof, of the pictures presented. Inwardly, he would be marveling at just how superior the photography was in comparison to Mohsin's efforts. The owner reserved two days of the week for the big shoot and, in the process, would do his own chatting up. He liked them young, in their early twenties, but, as he aged, so did his ability to attract this age group progressively diminish. But he did manage the odd pickings. In these cases, the lure of the owner of a modeling agency was simply too strong.

"These won't do. You'll have to have a fresh portfolio done with us. Our clients are very demanding."

And the portfolio-holder would leave, the blissful smile now vanished altogether or replaced by a tight-lipped one, and Max was certain that that was the last he would see of that person. He was right.

"Why do you charge so much?"

"Because we have to pay the lab, we take so many pictures of you and we add a mailing charge for sending them to all our clients. And we don't charge that much. Go to these places (and he would mention names) and see how much they charge!"

Max would not mention that the lab costs would be a small fraction of the price tag, that there never was going to be any mailing done and that the names he mentioned were highly professional studios where excellence of work commanded the lofty prices they charged.

"Then why don't you take out the money from our first paycheck? You can afford to."

This was a tough one and Max had the standard curt take-it-or-leave-it answer: "This company doesn't work that way."

And, on the portfolio day, an average of five young men and women would arrive with a large shoulder bag full of various attires, be made up by Natalie, have their pictures taken and fork out the 150 pounds (preferably in cash, but checks backed up by proper ID were acceptable). A week later they would be given a bunch of coloured and sepia-tinted (created in the lab from the colour negatives) pictures of indifferent to occasionally good quality. They could select a dozen for their own portfolio and then, to make everything appear businesslike, be made to sign a contract that would never go beyond the paper it was printed on. Then they were sent on their way with the promise that they would be contacted as soon as something turned up, or they could periodically call up or drop by to have a chat.

"Don't disappear!"

Most did — back to the country they came from. This was a crucial factor in Dream Face being able to continue its scam business. So many young tourists from, it seemed, every country in the world would descend on London and take immediate recourse to the weekly magazines without which life for the sojourner would be a little more trying in that city. Mohsin advertised in the most popular of those along the same lines as Max had seen in the Bengali-language newspaper, but with the omission of the adjective "Asian" from the print. He knew what he was doing and was perfectly aware of the psychology of the young readers. They would like to make a quick buck during their short stay and the advertisement sounded too good to pass up. Mohsin would joke about it to Max: "But they don't know that it's too good to be true," and end with a loud and long guffaw. Max would not join in the mirth, recalling his own gullibility, but would go along with a series of little nods of the head. The suckers would wait for the call that would never come and then leave London maybe a little wiser, 150 pounds lighter and with a portfolio of worthless photographs that were of questionable quality.

Some, however, did not disappear. They were mostly British or long-term visitors with temporary work permits. They would persist until they simply gave up. A few would turn nasty — Max once witnessed a particularly angry young man shove Mohsin hard — and the owner then would return the 150 pounds with his sincere apology and the comment, "I tried my best, but none of my clients showed any interest in your looks." Max was at first puzzled by the reference to clients. As he took on a bigger workload he would note that Mohsin would absent himself on several days outside of the portfolio days. Natalie would explain that he had gone to see the clients with pictures, including Max's. That pleased him, but, when after a while nothing came of those visits, he became baffled. Someone had to get an offer, for God's sake, but he kept his thoughts to himself. Later, when he unobtrusively became a part of the scam, he learnt that Mohsin stayed home or was doing his chores behind the lie of his client visits. By this time Mohsin trusted his manager so much that he made him his unofficial accountant. Then Max would also tell model-wannabes and models-scammed that the boss had gone for short stints to Paris, Milan or to any of the other fashion hotspots to hobnob with the big guns of the industry.

Max's conscience did bother him, but he could only mildly suggest to his boss if it would not be more profitable to garner clients.

"Too much work. This is easy money and we're also getting the girls!"

Max talked about his troubled conscience with Kenny.

"Stay on for a while and look for something else. Then leave."

Max was also getting restless for immigration. He remembered Kenny telling him that that the most convenient way to that arcadia would be to get married to a local woman.

"There are many Indians I know who would be willing to marry you."

The Western social customs of Great Britain are still not necessarily a bar to the age-old Eastern practice of arranged marriage. The fascinating aspect of this phenomenon is the willingness of South Asian women, born and brought up in Britain, to agree to their parents' choice of grooms. But Max had brushed aside that suggestion. It would put an end to his philandering ways. And he was not ready to settle down just yet. For a long period, therefore, he kept looking for a sponsoring godfather. Kenny was too busy looking for his own investing godfather to bother about beginning the arduous process of sponsoring him from his own company, that is, if he could at all do it. Max was beginning to feel the strenuous effects of continuously living life on the edge. He was seriously thinking of marriage as his salvation, but he still balked at settling for an arranged marriage. If he was going to tie the knot it was going to be through falling in love with a preferably white British woman. He was going on the lookout for one, but, dammit, there were all these model-wannabes to liaise with. Like the enchanting vision who was about to ensconce in front of him when the spoilsport Farukh Akbar loomed into his view and, worse, cheerfully announced his name and ended with "I've an appointment."

Eventually he had to call him.

"Fuck you! Why do I have to see you?" silently flashed through his mind. "So why do you want to become a model?" were the words that came out of his mouth. No, Max did not like him and he normally liked most people. The fellow sitting in front of him looked seventeen, but could be four or five years older. South Asians generally age gracefully and the men may look younger than they actually are. He also saw a slimly built small man, five and a half feet in height and very smartly and fashionably dressed. He was good looking, no doubt about that, with a smallish oval face a little marred by zits breaking out of a skin inclined to be oily. His sensuous mouth every so often broke out into dazzling smiles that revealed two rows of gleaming even white teeth. A long nose, just inclining towards an aquiline shape, gave Max the impression that he was of Pathan ethnicity. A pair of finely arched eyebrows framed two widely set, large chocolate-brown eyes that always seemed to be twinkling. These were his best features and conveyed an air of innocence about their owner, but, without him being able to pinpoint the reason, to Max they projected an aura of evil.

"This is weird. I must have gone bonkers thinking like that."

Nevertheless, the feeling persisted. He, however, had to acknowledge the beautifully groomed thick black hair, brushed back from a slightly sloping forehead and shaped into a ponytail at the back of his rather scrawny neck. And he oozed charm. Enough to pull Max back from an initial hostile outlook.

Farukh paid the ten quid for the test shots without any question, but perceptibly hesitated when informed about the portfolio cost. The smile left his face, and the twinkle from his eyes, replaced by an air of acute wariness. Max also perceived an aura of unspoken menace and he was kind of worried, but he soon dismissed it as the product of an overworked imagination.

Farukh made a final point: "Is it all right if I pay half on the day of the shoot and the rest when I collect my pictures? Also, will I get much work?"

"That can be arranged," was the confident answer to the first query. "I have no doubt that you will get a lot of work" was stated with a conviction that he did not feel and knew was hollow anyway. Somehow he felt like a fool saying it to this particular person. He had this idea that Farukh had already seen through the scam and was playing along to see where it would lead. Max had been right in one respect. Farukh did have Afghan parents, but they had migrated to the city of Mumbai in India a long time ago. He had been born there and had migrated to Holland through the sponsorship of his married elder sister and her husband who was a citizen of that country. He had come to England a few months ago.

Farukh came back to get his four test shots and paid the seventy-five pounds on the day of the portfolio shoot. He also came in with a couple of East European men in their late twenties who hardly spoke a word of English.

"My bodyguards," explained the young man, and Max took notice. Farukh's uncle had hired them for his safety.

"Your uncle?"

"He's my guardian," and mentioned a big name Bollywood movie producer who was also reported to be one of the most powerful bosses of India's underworld. "He's my father's younger brother. He's rented a house for me. I like it there, but sometimes I stay at his place in Gloucester Road."

Max knew about this uncle and was certain that he could afford the house in Gloucester Road.

"Does he live there?"

"Very little. Most of the time he lives in Dubai and Mumbai. He has two wives." Max was aware that Islam allowed multiple wives, but he could not figure out the significance of the remark.

"Why the bodyguards?"

"My uncle has many enemies. They might kidnap me to get at him. And my father also asked him to take good care of me."

Max was now very intrigued and asked him to come by on other days. He had formulated a Good Samaritan idea that he wanted to run by Farukh.

"I have this friend who is short of funds to make a movie. Do you think your uncle will be willing to help?" And filled in the details of Kenny's predicament.

"Let me talk to him first."

A few days later he came back and collected all his portfolio pictures, including the negatives, without paying the outstanding balance. He requested Max to write that off.

"Why? You have lots of money."

"I want to make it on my own, like my uncle. He doesn't give me that much. Thinks I'll be spoiled. Well, I'll show him."

Max was wondering about his wanting to take all the negatives.

"How will we print pictures to send to our clients?"

"I don't think I want to become a model. Oh, I talked with my uncle. He's in Dubai. He might be interested, but he wants to know more details."

And Max no longer questioned Farukh's decision to make off with all his pictures and negatives and had no problem in writing off the remainder of the money that he owed.

Kenny Rebeiro jumped at the idea after expressing initial reservations about the prospective financier's underworld reputation. Max coaxed him into seeing the positive benefits that he could gain from such an association. He was also looking at the decided advantages that he could obtain by his own tangential connection. A commission from the invested money was a distinct possibility, no, almost a certainty. Kenny would have to enlarge his production office staff, and he would surely not refuse Max an executive's position. That would necessarily entail arranging working papers for him. All the colours of the spectrum and all their radiant amalgamations twinkled in front of his eyes and pulsated inside his brain. So what if Farukh's uncle had an unsavoury reputation. Kenny did not have to deal with him at that level. He might not have to directly deal with him at all. Farukh could act on his uncle's behalf and Max would be there on his friend's. And, after all, the film investment was legitimate business. Ah, but it could very well be a channel to launder his dirty money. That was not his concern; he was going to be in possession of white money. Kenny gave in. And met Farukh. And Max was already counting the days before he would bid farewell to Mohsin Altaf and Dream Face. To begin life in Britain with the precious working permit. To finally come out of the shadows. He would miss Mohsin and the patsy models though. Oh well, he could always drop in to have a chat with the old boss and there would now be all those starlets to chat up. Best of all, he would not have to get hitched until he was ready to. Life was good.

Farukh had come to Kenny's office with one of his bodyguards, a short, sleepy-looking rotund man with a rolling gait who looked more convincing as a street derelict than as someone who could take care of someone's security. Max felt that one of his punches into his paunch would see him flopping about on his back, but maybe his appearance was deceptive and he was good at his job. Even then, if circumstances forced him, Max would have loved to have the fat man's face and tummy make a rude and painful acquaintance with his clenched fists. And seeing him come in brought back his original distaste, but in a watered-down version, of Farukh. Why did that little sonofabitch have to bring in an extra baggage? And forget that blather about his uncle's concern for his security. And all that talk about cars.

After the preliminary introductions, Farukh had a perfunctory discussion with Kenny about the monetary investment. He would get back within a few days. What kind of car did Kenny own? As it happened, he had a latest model maroon Jaguar and a white Mercedes sports convertible of a much earlier vintage. Kenny had a weakness for cars. Farukh had a fanatical obsession for them. He had come in a small decrepit dirty white car with two thin blue parallel lines running low along both sides, which seemed to have been procured from one of those dubious garages that did business in stolen vehicles. It belched noxious black fumes when started and Max wondered what in the world the ward of an immensely rich man was doing with a contraption like that.

"My uncle doesn't want me to have nice cars. So I bought this from my savings. But I want to have a brand new Jaguar."

He came back a few days later with another car of the same quality, probably procured from the same seedy garage, but of a flaked-off faded blue colour from which intermittent patches of off-white paint peeked out.

"This is my other car."

And to Kenny: "My uncle will finance the whole project, but he has set some conditions. You will give him the first week's profits from the film. If there is none, then he doesn't want any money back. He insists that you must have my name as a co-producer, but you cannot mention his name anywhere in the credits. If you agree, then he will give you the money in two installments, half in two weeks' time, the rest during the shooting, but on my recommendation."

Kenny played the seasoned businessman. "It sounds good, but let me think on it for a couple of days."

And, later, he let out his real feelings to Max. "I don't believe it! Ismail Merchant, move over. Kenny Rebeiro has arrived! Max, you will be my office manager."

And Max went to Dream Face to regretfully tender his oral resignation. He was a little peeved when Mohsin accepted it as a matter of routine and with a suspicion of relief in his voice.

"You're always welcome to drop in. And congratulations on your new job. Don't forget us when you become a big movie mogul." Then he added, "Your investor is a really big gangster. Be careful."

Max returned a month later to gloat to his old boss and Natalie about the progress of the big movie project. They were genuinely glad to see him and Natalie, in a moment of private conversation, expressed her desire to join the production company.

"I'll have to ask Kenny, but I'll put in a good word for you."

Mohsin learnt that it had been a progress of promises. No money had actually been handed over by Farukh.

"But he will soon."

Max returned a couple of months or so later. "Mohsin, can you take me to the lab?"

Kenny had placed him on his payroll for a modest compensation that only just exceeded his Dream Face salary, but had so far balked at filing for working papers for him.

"Once the first installment comes in, I'll give you a big raise and also begin the paper work for you. Hope you understand why I've to go slow."

Max was annoyed with Farukh. He was dangling the carrot in front of his and Kenny's eyes, just out of their reach, but tantalizingly just, enough to keep them slavering. There was a gamut of reasons: his uncle was making sure of Kenny's credibility, or he was in the middle of a delicate business deal, or he was in the process of releasing the funds. And all the time he kept talking about cars and his desire to own a brand new Jaguar. Then, one day, Kenny talked to the elusive man who was going to be his benefactor. So did Max. Farukh called up to say that his uncle was on a brief visit to London and would like to talk to them.

"Why don't you come for dinner tomorrow evening? I'm staying at my Gloucester Street home. I've instructed my accountant here to pay you the money."

And, then, to Kenny: "Farukh is a little wild. I'd be happy if you looked after him."

The riotous colours returned to Max's head, and his new boss invited him to a lavish dinner that very evening at the best Anglo-Indian restaurant in London. But they could not make it to the Gloucester Road dinner because the uncle called up the next morning to regret that he had to leave for Dubai that very evening. An important business meeting had come up, you know. Kenny understood, but was still disappointed. Next time, and don't worry, he would get his money soon. To make up for his sudden departure, he had authorized his accountant to hand him over the full amount asked for. He would handle the necessary documentation.

A few days later Farukh showed up to ask for a three thousand pound loan from Kenny to make a down payment on a Jaguar he wanted to purchase. Max was suspicious.

"Why don't you get the money from your uncle?"

"I told you he won't give it to me."

"How will you pay back?" was Kenny's query.

"Take it out from my fees as a producer."

This was news to both.

"I'm not going to work for nothing. I'll ask my uncle to tell you the amount."

Max's old resentment flared up. "Why can't you wait for a few days? The funds will be here soon."

"But this car might not be around."

Kenny settled the issue by agreeing to Farukh's request. And Max seethed inside with anger. And still there was no sign of the promised manna. Max called up Farukh who assured him that everything would be settled the following week. He was less than reassured.

"It better be."

The riposte was more soothing. "It will. We both stand to gain."

Max had taken a two-day break the week the money was supposed to have rolled in. He was doing an inventory of his apartment and making a list of the things that he needed to add to its fixtures. Electronic items headed the list. Things that he would soon be able to afford. He received a call from Kenny the second afternoon of his interlude.

"Farukh wants five thousand quid to pay off for his car."

"Don't give him. Wait, let me come over."

"But I've already given him the cash."

"You fool! You won't see the money again."

"But the big money will be here in a couple of days. He told me."

"Exactly. He told me too. But he didn't tell me he was going to you."

"Well, I had to gain the confidence of his uncle. Otherwise, he might have pulled out. Don't worry."

Max did worry. Suddenly, all his incipient feelings about Farukh came back, and this time they refused to go away. That week passed, the next one arrived, but there was no sign of any money or any word from Farukh. He had a mobile number. Max called only to find it switched off. He had given them an address in Hackney that neither had bothered to check out. Now they rushed there to find a rundown building which was opened to them by the ball-of-fat bodyguard.

"Yes, he used to live here, but he moved out two days ago."

"Where?"

"I don't know." Max was certain that he did, but was equally sure that he would not divulge it.

The two silently drove back to Kenny's office and only spoke once they had flopped down on their chairs. And Kenny unconsciously used a North Indian word for greed that his friends from that part and Pakistan often used.

"You see what *lallach* does to you. Why didn't I see it? No, I saw the signs, but ignored them for my *lallach*."

"I know. I should have noticed them."

Kenny turned on him, "It's your fault. You brought him over."

Max did not say anything. He was distraught, but recognized that his friend was upset even more. But when he persisted, Max could no longer remain silent.

"I warned you not to give him anything! And I didn't force you to deal with him."

They realized that accusing each other would get them nowhere. They talked it over and Max went back to his old boss. He only gave Mohsin a vague explanation about his request for taking him to the lab. They were in luck. Normally, test shot negatives, which did not go to Dream Face, were destroyed after a month by the lab to create storage space. As it happened, and only because Max could recall the exact date of their processing, they discovered the batch of negatives that included Farukh's miraculously still intact. Max requested several positives and only revealed to Mohsin that the young man had been missing for several days and that he was going to circulate those pictures among the police and the major local South Asian-language newspapers.

Kenny and Max did exactly that, and more. They went to the police, told their story of the swindling, and the officer recorded their statements, including Max's. Max was nervous, fearing that the police might find out about his own transgression and wished he did not have to testify. But realistically he could not do otherwise, not without undermining Kenny's case. Thank goodness, the investigating officer did not ask for his particulars outside of ascertaining that he was the person who introduced Farukh to Kenny. The major ethnic newspapers of London, Birmingham and Bradford were supplied the photos along with suggestion for write-ups. As a result, all the papers carried Farukh's face on their front pages along with a prominent storyline which reflected the captions that generally ran along these lines: "BEWARE OF THIS CON ARTIST." Max had a particular inner satisfaction in imagining that bastard's face when he saw them. He might want to go back to Holland or whatever hole he came out from. He must be a bastard son of the "uncle" by one of his maidservants. If he was not illegitimate then he must be a son of that "uncle's" numerous menservants.

Max was incensed at the thought that that pipsqueak could so easily outsmart them. He could almost imagine the lowlife's evil squirming brain all the while plotting his con game behind dazzling disarming smiles and sweet talk, and then laughing at his success in making a fool out of the two older men. He wanted to squash that filthy slimy squirming brain. And he, with Kenny's help, set about planning to do exactly that. They knew people in the South Asian community who would be willing to do them that favour. If not actually beat his brains out, at least give him a beating that would leave him a cripple. Max and Kenny settled for the last option as the safest.

They could not be charged with murder, and Farukh would not complain to the police about some goons roughing him up with more than a heavy hand. A few of the toughs had actually gone to Hackney in the hope of finding him, but he was not to be found, and they reassured the conned men of getting him very soon. The South Asian community numbered only so many and he would stick out in other ethnic groups.

As it happened, the police got to him first. Kenny told Max the details. Farukh had bought his Jaguar and had driven it to Hackney when plainclothes detectives who had banked on the theory that criminals often return to their familiar surroundings nabbed him. They had booked him, but were not sure how they could hold him. He had an ID card that showed him to be seventeen and, thus, a minor who was subject to special considerations. But he had numerous other cards and the police suspected they, along with the ID, were forgeries that they were going to investigate. They were hopeful of success and, then, Farukh would be in serious trouble. They could give no firm indication about the status of the car. But Kenny had told them that he would just be glad to see Farukh behind bars. And Max's brain was pulsating vigorously at the thought that the pretty boy could conceivably be repeatedly sodomized while in the slammer.

Then the euphoria died down and Kenny and Max were left to confront their situation. The lawful expatriate was philosophical about his financial loss because he knew that he was going to recoup that from his regular business, but stayed heartbroken for a long time over the bigger loss of his passionate dream. The illegal hardworking dreamer was in a turmoil of uncertainty. He was under no illusion about being retained at his job by Kenny and resolved to turn in his resignation without delay. Then? He had burnt his bridges with Mohsin and pride would not allow him to even go meet him and admit his failure in the movie industry. Natalie would commiserate, but Max was in no mood to be pitied. He could, and would, go back to the grind of the restaurants and the occasional pub and accounting house, but he would be back to square one with a bang. And he was not sure how long he could stomach staying there.